SOJOURNER TRUTH,
A Self-Made Woman

Also by Victoria Ortiz

The Land and People of Cuba

SOJOURNER TRUTH,
A Self-Made Woman

by Victoria Ortiz

J. B. Lippincott Company
Philadelphia and New York

Printed in the United States of America
First Edition

U.S. Library of Congress Cataloging in Publication Data

Ortiz, Victoria, birth date
Sojourner Truth, a self-made woman.

SUMMARY: A brief biography of the northern slave who after gaining her freedom became the first black woman to give antislavery lectures in the United States.
1. Truth, Sojourner, d. 1883—Juvenile literature. [1. Truth, Sojourner, d. 1883. 2. Abolitionists. 3. Negroes—Biography]
E185.97.T888 301.44′93′0924 [B] [92] 73-22290
ISBN-0-397-31504-X

For Bobbye: mother, sister, comrade

Acknowledgments

The author would like to express her gratitude to the following institutions for permission to reproduce the photographic material on the pages indicated:

Long Island Historical Society, 22

Michigan Historical Collections of the University of Michigan, 13, 38, 49, 90, 95, 97, 106, 110, 135, 142, 145, 148

New-York Historical Society, 56, 61, 64, 117

New York Public Library, 69, 84, 120

Sophia Smith Collection, Smith College, 77, 151

The author is especially grateful for access to the Berenice Bryany Lowe Papers concerning Sojourner Truth, housed in the Michigan Historical Collections; and for the help afforded her by the librarians at the Burton Historical Collection of the Detroit Public Library.

Contents

I can't read a book, but I can read the people

When the nineteenth century began, the United States was barely a quarter of a century old and was governed by its second president. It probably seemed to many that the new century would bring decades of tranquil growth and development to the new country. But the prospects for peaceful progress in the United States were severely limited by the realities of slavery. In fact, the nineteenth century was virtually defined by the violent relations between black and white, slave and slaveholder, dissenter and conservative.

It was a century of sharp divisions, focused on the issue of slavery. Soon many other issues became further reason for debate and battle. By the time the Civil War erupted in 1861, and from then into the twentieth century, the struggle for the abolition of slavery had sparked the fights for black suffrage, female suffrage, temperance, universal public education, racial integration, sexual equality, and many other causes. They all seemed to come together at the question of slavery and the hostilities it engendered: those who were for temperance and against war, for female equality and against child labor, were more than likely to be for emancipation and against slavery.

Among those who fought to end slavery, the black abolitionists were naturally the most determined and militant. There were also many white people whose dedication earned them places of high distinction beside their black co-fighters. Interestingly, it was often women who gave themselves over most ardently and tirelessly to the cause of the slaves. Defying centuries of ingrained prejudice, they carried their passionate truths to pulpits and platforms across the country and soon saw the close relationship between the enslavement of a whole ethnic group and the oppression of a whole sex.

In this century, characterized by the struggles of so many to liberate themselves and others, hundreds of figures emerged whose uniqueness and importance can never be overstated. Their names are legion: Frederick Douglass, Harriet Beecher Stowe, John Brown, Lucretia Mott, Dred Scott, Harriet Tubman, William Lloyd Garrison, Elizabeth Cady Stanton, Nat Turner, Susan B. Anthony, William Wells Brown, Laura Haviland, and so many others. The anonymous women and men who formed the bulk of the fighters can never be individually named, but they are nevertheless remembered.

Among the true patriots of this country is a black woman

whose life spanned almost the whole century; whose experience took in both slavery and freedom; who saw the North, the South, and the West; who lent her strong voice and muscular arm to the cause of both slave and freedman, man and woman. Widely hailed during her lifetime, Sojourner Truth has, in our century, received but a hint of the attention she deserves, for she truly embodied the period in which she lived, devoting herself fully to the struggle for liberty and justice for all in this country.

In a preface to Sojourner Truth's *Narrative*, her long-time friend and companion Frances Titus tells of the response of this tall, deep-voiced black woman to an allusion to Horace Greeley: "You call him a self-made man; well, I am a self-made woman." That, indeed, is what Sojourner was: from the raw material that was the slave known as Isabella, she made herself Sojourner Truth, a convinced and unshakable fighter for freedom. She made herself into a beloved and charismatic public speaker; she made herself into the friend and equal of great men and women; she made herself into a concerned and militant champion of the rights of her black sisters and brothers; she made herself into a warm-hearted, straight-backed, strong-willed, and steady-eyed woman who would not be turned from the road she chose to travel. A perceptive participant in the struggles of the period, she could truly say of herself. "I can't read a book, but I can read the people."

Her friend Joseph Dugdale declared: "No pen . . . can give an adequate idea of Sojourner Truth," and that is most likely true. But her colleague Parker Pillsbury wrote that "the wondrous experiences of that most remarkable woman would make a library, if not indeed a literature, could they all be gathered and spread before the world." We owe it to ourselves to read the literature of her wondrous experiences, because they will illuminate a great century and a great woman who was a part of it.

SOJOURNER TRUTH,
A Self-Made Woman

1.

I felt as if the power of a nation was with me

Unfortunately for her, Sojourner Truth was born two years too early. Probably sometime during 1797 the slave woman Elizabeth, property of Colonel Hardenbergh of Hurley, in New York's Ulster County, gave birth to a baby girl. The father of the child, James, was known as Baumfree, which in Low Dutch meant "tree," for he was tall and straight and muscular. Their daughter Isabella (she did not change her name to Sojourner until many years later) would have been guaranteed her freedom at the age of twenty-five, if she had been born after July 4, 1799; for in that year the New York State Legislature passed a decree granting eventual emancipation to some slaves. But as it was, the date of Isabella's birth cost her three precious years of freedom.

This law providing for eventual and selective emancipation reflected New York's ambivalence on the slavery issue. As early as

1652, when the state was the Dutch-ruled colony of New Amsterdam, the importation of African slaves had been permitted by law. When the British conquered New Netherland in 1664, the institution of slavery became fully entrenched in the state. By 1720 there were four thousand slaves in a total population of thirty-one thousand, making New York one of the northern states with the largest number of slaves.

In the North as well as in the South, slaves were chattels—movable, tangible property held by owners as are sheep, cows, or other livestock. At the whim of the master or mistress a slave would be well or badly used, and in most cases the treatment of slaves was far from gentle. So abused were the slaves in New York State that many incidents of attempted rebellion occurred. In 1741, in retribution for one of these early slave uprisings, New York settlers burned thirteen slaves, hanged eighteen, and shipped seventy others out of the area.

Not all New York residents, however, were so callous about the question of slavery, and by 1777 the antislavery forces were a clear majority in the state's first Constitutional Convention. More cautious than radical, they clamored for the eventual emancipation of the slaves, to take effect once the Revolutionary War was won. It was not until 1781, though, that the legislative body of New York State actually voted on any emancipation issue. In that year it was agreed to free those slaves who had been serving in the armed forces and fighting against the British.

From then on, the question of the abolition of slavery in New York continued to be approached piecemeal, for there were always some who feared immediate emancipation, and others who argued that slave owners should be compensated for their loss. In opposition were those who demanded immediate and uncompensated manumission of all slaves. The battle raged between the two factions for several decades. In the meantime, the year 1785 saw the passage of a bill forbidding the transportation of slaves into the state; in 1788 the slave trade was outlawed in New York; finally, in 1799, the legislature voted to free the children born after July 4 of that year—the women at age twenty-five, the men at twenty-eight. It was thus two years after Isabella was born that the total emancipation of New York's slaves began.

The slave child Isabella was unaware of the legal battles being waged on her behalf. Her childhood was touched very little by the changes the legislators had voted. Far more important to her early development were the things going on around her. Colonel Hardenbergh's death, for example, when she was an infant, meant that her first master was in fact the old man's son, Charles Hardenbergh. His family, descended from Dutch patroons and German nobility, was important in the region and in its time had owned two million acres of land granted by Queen Anne, had sat in the local congresses and assemblies, and had commanded the Ulster militia. Only fourteen years before Isabella was born, George Washington and his wife had visited the area and were entertained by the Hardenberghs in their manor house at Stone Ridge, a sturdy, imposing edifice of stone, tall-chimneyed and oak-beamed, built in 1672 by Louis Hardenbergh, son of the Espous Patroon of Holland.

The first dwelling Isabella recalled was not this manor, but rather the house that Charles Hardenbergh built upon inheriting the family estate. He had designed it as a hotel, showing little

Loaned by Albert Leffingwell. M.D. Brooklyn. New York

KNOW all Men by these Presents, THAT I Johannis Doxstader of Burnefield In the County of Albany

For and in Consideration of the Sum of Ninety Pounds Current Money of the Province of New York to me in Hand paid at and before the Ensealing and Delivery of these Presents, by Jacob Cuyler of the City of Albany the Receipt whereof I do hereby acknowledge, and myself to be therewith fully satisfied, contented, and paid: HAVE Granted, Bargained, Sold, Released, and by these Presents do fully, clearly and absolutely grant, bargin, sell and release unto the said Jacob Cuyler. a Negro Named Har. about Eighteen years old

To HAVE and to HOLD the said Negro Named Har unto the said Jacob Cuyler His Eyres and Executors, Administrators, and Assigns, for ever. And I the said Joh. Doxstader for my Self, my Heirs, Executors and Administrtors, do covenant and agree to and with the above-named Jacob Cuyler His Executors, Administrators and Assigns, to warrant and defend the Sale of the above-named Negro Har against all Persons whatsoever. IN WITNESS whereof I have hereunto set my Hand and Seal, this Twelveth Day of October Anno q. Dom. One Tousand Seven Hundred ~~and Fifty~~ Sixty three

Sealed and Delivered in the Presence of

George Smith

[illegible]

Johan. his + mark Dachstader

Negro Slavery in New York State

A bill of sale for a negro. Price - £90. - Date Oct 12th 1763 -

Presented to - The Long Island Historical Society - by Albert Leffingwell

Bill of sale for a slave sold in New York State in the eighteenth century concern for providing comfortable shelter for his slaves. Crowded together, the men, women, and children who made up Charles Hardenbergh's property shared the hotel's dank, evil-smelling cellar. Here, where the floor was so loosely constructed that the dampness and vapors from the muddy foundations just below filled the room, the slaves slept. "She shudders, even now," reads Sojourner's dictated *Narrative*, "as she goes back in memory, and revisits this cellar, and sees its inmates, of both sexes and all ages, sleeping on those damp boards, like the horse, with a little straw and a blanket."

Isabella's mother, affectionately called Mau-mau Bett, cared for her daughter as well as she could, ingraining in her the proper balance of independence and obedience necessary for a child to survive in the cold and unpredictable world of slavery. She taught her the importance of doing her master's will, lest she provoke his wrath and be whipped or otherwise abused. She also taught young Isabella her first prayers, lisped by the child in Low Dutch, the first language she learned.

In later years, Sojourner was able to conjure up scenes of family closeness: huddled together with Isabella around a burning pine knot, which provided a weak but glowing light, Mau-mau Bett and Baumfree would tell stories, sing, or otherwise instruct their daughter. But many of these memories are tinged with the tragedy of separation and violence. Sojourner remembered hearing about the winter day on which her brother and sister were taken away from their mother on a sled, never to be seen by her again. When the memories became too painful, Sojourner recalled, her mother would groan and sigh, and, looking up at the stars, would say:

"Those are the same stars, and that is the same moon, that look down upon your brothers and sisters, and which they see as they look up at them, though they are ever so far away from us, and each other."

By the time Isabella was about nine years old, the slave population of New York and New Jersey had reached over thirty-six thousand, and the lawmakers of New York were still arguing about how and when to abolish slavery. In 1806 things on the Hardenbergh estate changed quite suddenly. Charles died, and all the property was up for auction, including his "slaves, horses, and other cattle." Nine-year-old Isabella faced for the first time what her older brothers and sisters had already experienced: separation from her parents. Bett and Baumfree were doubly fearful, for there was a chance that they too would be separated. But by that time Baumfree, once so tall and proud, was old, half-blind, and stooped and twisted by rheumatism. The Hardenbergh heirs decided that the most expedient solution was to free Mau-mau Bett and Baumfree, so the two old people could care for each other. They could continue to live in the miserable cellar, but they would be forced to find their own living since they were no longer the family's charges.

Isabella, however, was young and marketable, although there is a story that her second master only bought her because she came with a flock of sheep. Whatever the truth of this was, it is known that John Neely, a storekeeper from Twaalfskill, bought her for one hundred dollars. Speaking only the Low Dutch of her former owners, Isabella suffered with this new English-speaking family and often misinterpreted Mrs. Neely's instructions. She was punished for these errors by her mistress, who considered her simply disobedient. She also recalled being beaten by Neely with rods tied together, and suffering from frozen feet during the winter months since he gave her no shoes.

Her parents, in the meantime, were making out poorly, for both were ill and aged and found little on which to subsist. Too soon, the stronger of them, Mau-mau Bett, died suddenly from "a fit of palsy," leaving her husband totally destitute. Isabella and her brother Peter were permitted by their respective masters to attend their mother's funeral and visit with their father. The poor man was stunned by his loss, crying out: "Oh, I had thought God would take me first—Mau-mau was so much smarter than I, and could get about and take care of herself—and I am *so old,* and *so helpless.* What *is* to become of me? I can't do anything more—my children are all gone, and here I am left helpless and alone." Isabella could do nothing about this family tragedy, despite her greater strength and youth.

Isabella spent about two years with the harsh Neely, and then, in what she later called a direct answer to a desperate prayer, she was purchased for $105 by a fisherman and innkeeper named Martin Schryver. Now her luck was better, as the Schryvers, although uncouth and uneducated, were warm people and treated her well. Her life with them took her often into the fields, for they had a farm, and Isabella "was expected to carry fish, to hoe corn, to bring roots and herbs from the woods for beers, go to the Strand for a gallon of molasses or liquor as the case might be, and 'browse around,' as she expresses it."

Isabella lived for about a year and a half with the Schryvers, and in 1810 was sold for seventy pounds (three hundred dollars) to John J. Dumont of New Paltz Landing. At the age of about thirteen, Isabella went to work for the family that was to own her until her freedom. They called her Bell, and her life with them was a mixture of good and bad, for while Mr. Dumont was quite kind and fair with her, his wife was strict and critical. Bell frequently displeased her mistress and recalled being scolded and punished for several mornings in a row because she allegedly had not washed the breakfast potatoes. With the help of the Dumonts' daughter Gertrude, Bell was finally cleared of guilt in the matter when it was revealed that Kate, the white serving girl, had put ashes in the potatoes while the pot was untended, in order to get the slave into trouble, to "grind her down" as Isabella put it.

Isabella lived with the Dumonts for seventeen years, growing into a tall, thin, tough young woman. Her physical strength was great, and John Dumont was wont to boast of her to his friends, saying that she "is better to me than a *man*—for she will do a good family's washing in the night and be ready in the morning to go into the field, where she will do as much at raking and binding as my best hands." In fact, she worked extra hard precisely to please her master, for she had come to believe that Dumont was like God—that he could see all she did and know all she thought, just as God could, and that any transgression on her part would bring his anger down on her. She strove to do more than he asked in order to receive his praise, and when she disobeyed him or misbehaved, she often confessed it to him before being discovered, so convinced was she of his omniscience.

For some time Isabella was involved in a relationship with a young slave named Bob, whose master, Catlin, lived nearby. Catlin looked with great disfavor on a union between the two young people, for any children born from it would automatically remain with the mother, thus becoming Dumont's property, and Catlin preferred to breed his slaves among his own slave women. Forbidden to see Isabella again, Bob nevertheless went to visit her once when she was ill; he was followed by Catlin and his two sons, who knocked the young man to the ground and were beating him brutally when Dumont rushed out and called on them to stop. He ordered them off his property, crying that he would have no "niggers" killed there; he then accompanied the men and their bleeding and bound slave to their farm, to make sure the young man was not further abused.

Dumont was also more generous than most slave owners when he allowed Isabella to visit with her old father on a few occasions. More and more decrepit, Baumfree was finally left in the care of Mau-mau Bett's brother Caesar and his wife Betty. But they were themselves extremely frail and advanced in years, and they soon died, leaving Baumfree completely alone in an isolated wooden shack. The last person to see him described him as being filthy, vermin-ridden, and very ill; when his body was found, it was clear he had either starved or frozen to death. The remaining Hardenberghs donated a plain pine coffin, black paint with which to stain it, and a jug of whiskey for the wake. The Hardenberghs probably considered this a more than ample reward for his years of labor.

In 1817, when Isabella had been with Dumont seven years, the New York State Legislature passed a law which granted eventual emancipation to all slaves born *before* July 4, 1799. Finally Isabella could dream of freedom, although the law also stipulated that they were to become free only as of July 4, 1827, ten years later. This meant that not only she, but also her children, would one day be free. Around 1814 Dumont had decided that Isabella was of breeding age, and he picked his slave Thomas as her mate. Subsequently she had five children by him, four of whom survived. The eldest, Diana, was born around 1815, and was to be the child who most closely resembled her mother. In the ten years following, Isabella bore Peter, Elizabeth, and Sophia. Of her husband, Thomas, little is known, since Sojourner herself rarely referred to him in her later years. It is known that after he was emancipated—Isabella had long since left him and the Dumont farm—he spent his last years in the poorhouse, where he died.

As July 4, 1827, drew closer, Isabella began to prepare herself for freedom. Dumont seemed to approve of the new statute and even promised to free her a year early if she worked well. However, when 1826 came, he withdrew his offer, claiming that the time Isabella lost during an illness had to be made up before she could be free.

This was perhaps the first time the young woman, already close to thirty, saw her master for what he was. Later, as she was dictating her *Narrative*, she exclaimed, on recalling Dumont's broken promise: "Ah! these slave holders are terrible for promising you this or that, or such and such a privilege, if you will do thus and so; and when the time of fulfillment comes, and one claims the promise, they, forsooth, recollect nothing of the kind; and you are, like as not, taunted with being a liar; or, at best, the slave is accused of not having performed his part or condition of the contract."

Her eyes now open to the real motives of her master, Isabella felt no qualms at leaving him before the law permitted. With her infant daughter Sophia on one arm and a bundle of belongings on the other, she walked across the hills early one morning, toward an unknown but attractive future of freedom.

It was really only at the age of about thirty that this woman, close to six feet tall and imposing in appearance, began to make herself into the Sojourner Truth who was eventually to be so well known. Before freedom was spoken of, the slave woman Isabella had been obedient, uncomplaining, and deeply religious, and had even believed "that slavery was right and honorable." So aquiescent was she to all the demands of her master that her fellow slaves on Dumont's farm referred to her as a "white man's nigger" and taunted her with being a fool for always obeying. But the promise of early freedom and the breach of that promise seem to have begun the change in her, a change clearly attested to by her determined departure that morning late in 1826. The strength and independence of spirit that she began to display were to characterize her until the day of her death.

With a new sense of decisiveness, Isabella proceeded to the home of a man named Levi Rowe, whom she remembered as being kind and sympathetic. Although deathly ill, the old man gladly directed the escaping slave and her baby to the home of Mr. and Mrs. Van Wagener, who welcomed her and urged her to stay. Soon Dumont arrived, angry and anxious to take her back with him.

When she refused to go, he threatened to take the child. Of course, by law she would soon have been free; but to make sure, Van Wagener agreed to pay twenty dollars for Isabella and five for Sophia, although he made it quite clear he did not approve of buying and selling human beings. Now Isabella was free from Dumont and in the home of a couple who would not allow her to address them as Master and Mistress and who urged her to sleep on the bed rather than under it, as was the custom with domestic slaves.

Shortly before Isabella's departure from Dumont's farm, her son Peter, then five, had been sold to a Dr. Gedney, friend and neighbor of the Dumonts. At the time Isabella had not worried, since it was understood that as soon as July 4, 1827, dawned, the boy would become free, as would his sisters and his mother. However, when she was living at the Van Wageners', she learned that Dr. Gedney, who had wanted Peter as a valet during a trip to England, had found the boy too young and had sold him to his brother Solomon Gedney; the brother, in turn, finding no use for the child, had sold him to his brother-in-law, a wealthy Alabama planter named Fowler, who had taken the boy to the South. Although the law expressly forbade the sale of any slave for transportation out of the state, the practice was common and generally could not be successfully contested.

But the Gedneys and Fowler had not bargained for the new, independent, and stubborn Isabella. When she heard what had happened to her son, she walked to New Paltz to find the man who had sold him South. Coming to the Dumonts' place, she went in to see if they could explain their complicity in the matter. Mrs.

Dumont heard her complaint and mockingly responded: "Ugh! a fine fuss to make about a little nigger! Why, haven't you as many of them left as you can see to and take care of? . . . Making such a halloo-balloo about the neighborhood, and all for a paltry nigger!"

Outraged to her deepest being, Isabella at that moment determined that she absolutely would get her son back. "Oh, my God! I knew I'd have him again," she recalled many years later. "I was sure God would help me to get him. Why, I felt so tall within—I felt as if the power of a nation was with me." And with that, Isabella, illiterate and poor, newly free and inexperienced in many of the ways of the white world, went about freeing her boy.

She first went to question Mrs. Gedney, mother of the man who had so abused Peter. Like Mrs. Dumont, this old woman mocked Isabella's anguish, laughingly pointing out to her that she, too, had lost her child to Fowler; for her daughter Eliza had married the man and was living in Alabama with him.

From there Isabella walked to Kingston, where some Quakers whom she had not known before were so moved by her tale that they offered to help her. On their advice, Isabella went to the Kingston courthouse and, after questioning all whom she met there, located the grand jury and presented her complaint. A lawyer, Esquire Chipp, agreed to help her through the intricacies of the law, and he drew up a writ which was to be served on Solomon Gedney.

Once again Isabella walked the fifteen miles between Kingston and New Paltz, where she delivered the writ to the constable. He promised he would serve it in all haste, but unfortunately he handed the writ to Gedney's brother, and in that way warned the real culprit, who escaped across the river and consulted there with his lawyer. Since he faced a possible fourteen years in jail for having sold the boy out of state, it was resolved that Solomon Gedney would return to Alabama and fetch Peter, and the case would be contested in Kingston once he returned with him. This was not, however, until the spring, several months later, and by that time Isabella was more than impatient.

On learning that she might have to wait even longer, since the court session was almost over, Isabella sought and found another lawyer, Esquire Romeyn, who promised to deliver her son to her within twenty-four hours if she gave him five dollars. Almost running to her Quaker friends nearby, Isabella managed to collect more than he had requested and gave it all to him. She felt that "if five dollars will get him, more will *surely* get him."

True to his word, Romeyn produced Peter the next evening, and the boy, in the company of Solomon Gedney, faced his mother in the presence of a judge. Probably terrified by the whole experience, Peter at first clung desperately to Gedney, whimpering that he did not want to leave him, that it was not his mother standing before him, that he loved his present master. The judge questioned him carefully and in the end ruled that the boy be returned to his mother. Tearfully the child approached her, mistrustful still. It took Isabella, the lawyer, and the court clerks to convince him at last that he was safe, that no one would take him back to Fowler. Only then did he accept Isabella as his mother.

Embracing and examining the boy, Isabella soon saw that his little body was covered from head to toe with the scars of many brutal beatings. Angrily she cursed his harsh master, calling on her God to "render unto them double." As she exclaimed in sadness over the welts on Peter's back, the child told her: "This is nothing, mammy. If you would see Phillis, I guess you'd scare. She had a little baby, and Fowler cut her till the milk as well as blood ran down her body. You would scare to see Phillis, mammy."

Hoping now to begin building a life in freedom, Isabella took Peter back with her to the Van Wageners', not realizing at that moment what an extraordinary thing she had just accomplished. Relying primarily on her own determination, she, a black woman, had taken a white man to court and had won her case against him. In 1828 that was almost unheard of. For Isabella it was further proof of God's bounty that she had finally rescued Peter from his bondage, for she had prayed hard as well as fought for him. And her God *did* seem to be working for her, for a few months later she learned that the Alabamian Fowler had gone berserk and brutally murdered his young wife, Eliza, the daughter of Mrs. Gedney who had mocked Isabella's pain. Recalling that she had asked Him to render unto her enemies double, Isabella guiltily told Him: "Oh, my God! That's too much—I did not mean quite so much, God!"

2.

It was God all around me

Sojourner Truth became aware of God's presence and that of Jesus Christ at one particular moment, a moment she remembered later in all its vivid images and sensations. She felt a strange fiery force, Sojourner declared, one day when she was still a slave; "It was God all around me, I could feel it burning, burning all around me, and going through me, and I saw I was so wicked it seemed as if it would burn me up." And as she sensed something or someone stepping between her and God's wrath, she realized that it was Jesus, "and then the whole world grew bright, and the trees they waved and waved in glory, and every little bit of stone on the ground shone like glass; and I shouted and said, 'Praise, praise, praise to the Lord!' And I began to feel such a love in my soul as I never felt before—love to all creatures."

This vision was by no means a unique, isolated experience, for from her young womanhood Isabella had gone through many moments of intense religious exaltation. At all moments her faith, which was based upon a very personal interpretation of Christianity, ruled her thoughts and actions. While too pragmatic at heart to become a mystic, Isabella and later Sojourner never lost the spiritual quality of her vision.

Her faith was always colored by a good dose of common sense and practicality, and the religious imagery in her speeches was more often than not rooted in the real world. She recalled that when she was a child God had reality for her only when she saw Him as a great figure like Washington or Lafayette. Jesus, when she finally learned of Him, was someone entirely separate, about whom she even asked: "Is he married?" She literally spoke to God when she prayed, finding an isolated corner of a field in order to speak in a loud voice to Him—the louder she called, the more likely He was to hear her. Later on, as she became better acquainted with the ways of organized religion, she modified these old habits a bit, but it seems that the early view of God as someone of whom one asked favors directly always remained with Sojourner. She was famous for beginning her public addresses with the phrase: "Children, I speak to God and God speaks to me . . ." and often claimed to have a direct line to His attention.

Even when she was still Isabella, this ardently religious and profoundly trusting woman became known in her small circle of friends as someone with a special gift for prayer. When she first moved to New York City, taking along her only son Peter (in about 1829), she joined the Methodist Church on John Street. Although technically a racially integrated church, it was the practice there as in other churches to separate the black and white congregations. No doubt this policy caused Isabella some uneasiness, for she was soon attracted to the Zion African Church on Church Street, an all-black institution where she felt more welcome. Here she was revered for her lengthy and eloquent prayers, and her singing, too, was admired and encouraged.

During the early period of her affiliation with the Zion Church Isabella met a brother and sister of hers, long ago sold away from the Hardenbergh estate. The brother, Michael, was the child who was featured in the incident Baumfree and Mau-mau Bett had recounted so often, about a wailing boy being taken away on a cold winter's day. Now, thirty-odd years later, Isabella met him again, through their sister Sophia, whom she had met at the Zion Church.

The most important thing that happened to Isabella in New York City was her involvement with the religious fanatic Matthias and his followers, and her subsequent tangling with the law. Through James Latourette, one of her first employers in the city, Isabella became involved with a group of "respectable females" who went about the seamier neighborhoods attempting the spiritual salvation of their "fallen sisters," the prostitutes who swarmed the New York slums. Inspired at first by their zeal, Isabella accompanied them and found pleasure in the occasional victories: a young woman would decide to go with them to the Magdalene Asylum on Bowery Hill, or a prayer meeting would be held on the very premises of one of the "houses of vice."

Soon, however, Isabella tired of the loud and hysterical prayer meetings held in the Latourette house and was happy to go and work for Elijah Pierson, a man whom she met at her employers' home. Finding him of a highly mystical nature, Isabella listened carefully to what he said about his spiritual experiences, chief among which was the revelation which had come to him on June 20, 1830, during a bus ride in the city: "He assumed the title of Prophet, asserting that God had called him in an omnibus in these words: 'Thou art Elijah, the Tishbite. Gather unto me all the members of Israel at the foot of Mount Carmel'; which he understood as meaning the gathering of his friends at Bowery Hill."

Much struck by his vehemence, Isabella was moved to believe his claims, and grew to admire him greatly, imitating him in all he did. This included fasting, an activity in which Pierson frequently indulged, claiming that it brought light to his spirit and made him see God's way more clearly. Hoping to become enlightened herself, Isabella went three days and three nights without eating; getting up on the fourth day, she was so weak that she fell to the floor. She then went to find something to eat, but not wanting to appear a glutton in God's eyes, she took only dry bread and water. On recalling this solitary experience with voluntary fasting, Sojourner pointed out that "she did get light, but it was all in her body and none in her mind—and this lightness of body lasted a long time. Oh! she was so light, and felt so well, she could 'skim around like a gull.' "

Soon the Pierson household was visited by a man named Robert Matthews, known better as Matthias. In his mid-forties, he had left his wife and children in upstate New York and had traveled through the state; by the time he reached the city he had already established his reputation as something of a mystic or, to some, a fanatical impostor. But he and Pierson seemed to take to each other, finding out, for example, that both had had revelations from God on June 20: Pierson had been designated Elijah the Tishbite, and, far away, Matthews had been enlightened and told to let his beard grow, as all true Christians refused to shave their chins. At that first meeting between the two men it was decided that Pierson was John the Baptist and Matthias God on earth, an agreement which was sealed with mutual foot-washing and much religious testifying.

Through all of this Isabella behaved most ingenuously,

On this scrap of paper Sojourner Truth had a friend record the date she found Jesus.

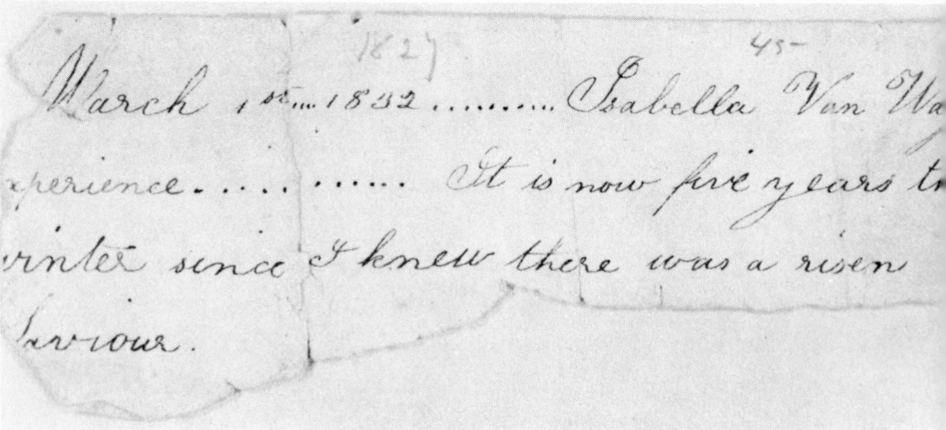

1827 45-

March 1st.... 1832 .... Isabella Van Wa

xperience. .... It is now five years t

vinter since I knew there was a risen

aviour.

throwing in her lot with these odd men and even turning over to Pierson all her savings, accumulated carefully with weekly deposits in a local bank. Eventually, readily convinced by Matthias himself—for whom she now worked—that the "Kingdom" that he and his followers were forming needed her participation, Isabella moved with them in 1833 to Sing Sing, New York, and there witnessed the Kingdom in its full glory. In the *Narrative*, her first biographer did not "deem it useful or necessary to give any particulars," but subsequent authors have revealed in greater or lesser detail the outrageous occurrences which took place in the Matthias household. These included the worship of Matthias as the Father, God on earth, and the granting to him of all the favors and privileges appropriate to such an elevated position; the use of everyone else's money for the benefit of the Kingdom, or more specifically Matthias himself; the employment of Isabella's housekeeping services without salary; wife-swapping, under the guise of uniting divinely designated "match-spirits," whether or not they coincided with already existing unions; communal mixed bathing, no doubt for purely spiritual purposes, and the like.

Isabella was able to avoid involvement in the more sordid aspects of the Kingdom. The only black person in the household, she was generally employed in her capacity as servant, and more often than not was ignored when it came to the more bizarre forms of worship required of all other members of the clan. She did, however, observe much of the strange behavior of her coreligionists, and while her loyalty did not waver, it did happen that her blind faith in Matthias and Pierson was somewhat diminished as their actions became more and more peculiar.

Pierson's death finally burst the bubble, bringing in its wake the arrest of Matthias on the charge of having murdered his one-time associate and rumors that somehow Isabella, referred to in the papers only as "the colored woman," had been involved as well. These events were as important to Isabella's development as her master John Dumont's broken promise had been, for now she saw that her white employers were capable of turning against her at the slightest pretext. This case involved the Folgers, a couple with whom she had lived at Sing Sing during the days of the Kingdom. Now that the strange community was breaking up and Ann Folger was no longer Matthias's favorite mistress, she and her husband claimed that Isabella not only was implicated in Pierson's death but had also attempted to poison the entire Folger family. In response to this accusation, after Matthias's case was closed and the man voluntarily exiled to the West, Isabella hired a lawyer and filed a slander suit against Folger.

With the same stubbornness and determination she had displayed when she demanded Peter's return from Alabama, Isabella pursued the reestablishment of her good name and reputation as far as she could. She walked miles and miles to request from friends and former employers statements attesting to her moral and personal integrity. All her employers praised her honesty, her industry, and her responsibility: John Dumont "always found her to be perfectly honest"; Isaac Van Wagener said "she was a faithful servant, honest and industrious"; and Mrs. Whiting of Canal Street in New York declared, "I do state unequivocally that we never have had a servant that did all her work so faithfully, and one in whom we could place such implicit confidence. In fact, we did, and do still, believe her to be a woman of extraordinary moral purity."

The New York newspapers, on the other hand, were filled with the lurid details of the Matthias case and did not hesitate to link Isabella's name to the affair. Nevertheless, she was not arrested and so was able freely to pursue the preparation of her slander suit. She was helped in this by a man named Gilbert Hale, whose interest in the Matthias household and the Kingdom had led him to Isabella. Convinced of her honesty and innocence in the death of Pierson, he assisted her greatly by publishing, in 1835, a two-volume work entitled *Fanaticism: Its Source and Influence, Illustrated by the Simple Narrative of Isabella.* In this work he praised the black woman's integrity and openness and declared that "she had shrewd common sense, energetic manners, and apparently despises artifice." Evidence in her favor far outweighed anything the vengeful Folgers could manufacture, and Isabella was awarded the sum of $125 by the court, to be paid by Folger for the damage he had caused to her good name.

Now that she was dissociated from the Kingdom, Isabella was able to devote herself to her son Peter, who was by that time about fourteen. During the years he had been growing to adolescence, his mother had been much too involved in her experience with religious fanaticism to see that he was spending more and more time with friends of questionable character. The big-city atmosphere of New York and the boy's natural curiosity and inexperience had led him to participate in activities which frequently brought him into conflict with the law. When he was arrested,

Isabella would always come to his aid, attempting to guide him and draw a moral lesson from his experience. She would take him back home with her, readily convinced that he would improve his conduct and leave his worthless friends.

However, Peter continued to see them and so continued to get into trouble. He often lied to his mother and to the friends who tried to help him. In one case, having been hired as a coachman, he went so far as to sell the livery his new employer had provided for him. When a friend of his mother's gave him ten dollars with which to pay for his training at a navigation school, Peter merely handed the money to the teacher and left, giving some excuse as to why he could not attend the classes.

Isabella finally gave up and decided no longer to live with her son, hoping that living on his own would force him to take better care of himself and to choose his companions more carefully. But once again he was arrested, and as usual he sent for his mother to help him. This time Isabella refused, and in desperation Peter called for Peter Williams, a black barber whose name he had been using in his life of petty crime. The barber was intrigued by this young man who had borrowed his name and went to see him in prison. Impressed by Peter's intelligence and quick wit, Williams agreed to help him. They went together to visit Isabella, and to her delight the barber promised that he would find a whaler on which the boy could ship out. Within a week Peter had signed up as a crew member on the *Zone*, and shortly thereafter, in 1839, he sailed, leaving Isabella greatly relieved. During the next two years she received three letters from him, and after that heard no more. She never found out what finally became of her son Peter.

With Matthias happily out of the picture and Peter at sea, Isabella was able to devote herself fully to the restructuring of her life. All her savings had been lost with the collapse of the Matthias Kingdom, and she had no money beyond what she earned from day to day. At this period Isabella began to look upon money and worldly property with distrust, for she had seen too many people who in her opinion forgot to live by God's laws in their pursuit of personal wealth. Even she had profited at the expense of others, she came to feel, for every job that she did seemed to be taking work away from someone who needed it even more than herself. One day, for instance, a man gave her half a dollar and told her to pay someone to clear the snow from in front of his house. Rather than pay someone else, Isabella did the job herself and kept the money. She immediately felt guilty about this, for she did not believe that she really needed it.

Looking around her at how people lived in New York, she said astutely: "Truly, here the rich rob the poor and the poor rob each other." The realization that she was just as guilty of selfish living as those whom she criticized led Isabella finally, in 1843, to set out from the city and leave behind her the kind of existence which it forced upon its population. She sensed that there were great things ahead for her if only she would follow the voice that told her to proceed east to Long Island, doing God's work as she traveled.

3.

When I left the house of bondage, I left everything behind

In the spring of 1843 Isabella packed her few belongings in a pillowcase and, taking only two shillings, she prepared to leave New York. She gave her employer, Mrs. Whiting, an hour's notice, explaining that she was going east because "the Spirit calls me there and I must go." On foot, and with only the sun as her guide, Isabella set out, taking the ferry over to Brooklyn. From there she walked eastward, ready to encounter almost any kind of future.

It was during the early part of her trip that the idea for a new name came to her, as she was later to recall: "My name was Isabella; but when I left the house of bondage, I left everything behind. I wasn't going to keep anything of Egypt on me, and so I went to the Lord and asked him to give me a new name. And the Lord gave me Sojourner, because I was to travel up and down the land, showing the people their sins, and being a sign unto them."

To a curious Quaker woman whom she met on her journey, she explained that her last name was always that of her master, and this had given her the idea for her new last name: since the Lord was her master, and His name was truth, she would name herself Sojourner Truth.

Thus, Isabella became Sojourner Truth on a highway about five miles from the ferry landing in Brooklyn, on June 1, 1843. It was a significant change, for with this early walk the stately black woman was beginning a new stage in her life, one which was to be more public and significant than the period that had gone before. Although she was about forty-six years old, she was strong and healthy, and her keen mind and great curiosity were to enable her to become involved in activities and ways of living which at that moment, walking east, she could not have even imagined.

She made her way across Long Island, taking odd jobs here and there if she needed to. Once a man stopped her and asked if she wanted work; although she had not been seeking any at that moment, she went along with him. There was someone ill in his family, and she gently nursed this person back to health. Sojourner won the family's gratitude and love, and they begged her to stay with them, but her feet longed to continue their journey. She felt she still had work to do that was more important than serving and nursing; she felt she was doing God's work.

This entailed more and more "preaching," as she called it. For now Sojourner began to acquire a name for herself as a compelling preacher and speaker, whose ability to hold an audience and often move them to tears was envied by many better-educated orators. She enjoyed public speaking, for she was always ready to tell God's truths and thereby do her duty toward Him. She also admitted to having "a good time" when she faced a large audience, and this open pleasure in being the center of attention was to remain with her all her life. While she could quote from the Bible, she later told friends, "When I preach I have just one text to preach from, and I always preach from this one. *My* text is 'When I found Jesus.' "

A month after setting out from New York, Sojourner reached Huntington and then Cold Springs, just in time to participate in the preparations for celebrating July Fourth. She cooked "New York" dishes for the mass temperance meeting which was to be held and earned the admiration and respect of all whom she met there. But even new friends could not hold her, and she continued on her travels, taking a boat to Bridgeport, Connecticut, and going from there to New Haven. All along the way she attended all prayer meetings she encountered, speaking as she was moved to do. She also began calling her own meetings, and soon those who had heard her preach in one place begged her to do so in another community, to another crowd. She went to Bristol and Hartford, at each place being recommended to friends of the people she had met in her earlier audiences.

In the meantime, since her three daughters—who were still living on the Dumont farm—had not been informed of Sojourner's whereabouts, they began to worry, and even wondered if their mother's disappearance from New York was an indication that she had become "a wandering maniac" or had killed herself. Sensing that her daughters might be concerned, Sojourner had a friend in Berlin, Connecticut, write to them, and from that day forth she kept in close and loving touch with them.

Her religious experiences in New York had taught Sojourner caution where strange sects and highly individualized biblical interpretations were involved. Thus, when she met people who believed in the "Second Advent," the immediate reappearance of Jesus Christ, she was curious enough to listen and watch but was always somewhat skeptical of their doctrines. She appreciated it when they encouraged her own preaching and was taken by their warmheartedness, but the agitation and noise which surrounded their religious ceremonies reminded her too much of the Matthias rites. With sharp wit she criticized them, pointing out that "the Lord might come, move all through the camp, and go away again," and they would never notice it because of all the noise and commotion!

Sojourner became a much-sought-after lecturer, and those who heard her were quick to praise her. A friend in Springfield, Massachusetts, described her demeanor before audiences: "When she arose to speak in their assemblies, her commanding figure and dignified manner hushed every trifler into silence, and her singular and sometimes uncouth modes of expression never provoked a laugh, but often were the whole audience melted into tears by her touching stories."

Her friends in Springfield took her eventually to the Northampton Association, a utopian settlement and community in Massachusetts. The association was dedicated to the promotion of freedom and equality in everyday living, and all who chose to join contributed equally to the advancement of these ideals. The community supported itself by the breeding of silkworms and the manufacture of silk. Everyone contributed labor, with no special privileges based on education or station in life. Here Sojourner stayed for a few years, thinking that perhaps she would be happy to settle among the high-minded and humanitarian people she found there. She soon came to like the atmosphere, although at first she had found the factory and living quarters too crowded and noisy. But, looking at all the good people around her, she thought that if they could live there, then so could she.

The Northampton experience was a seminal one for Sojourner, for there she first met men and women who were active in the abolitionist movement and in other struggles for social change. She was moved by the freedom allowed to all who lived there and was able to recognize the value of living and behaving as a Christian, not merely believing as one. She met people of differing religious persuasions—among them Quakers, Methodists, and Adventists, and even some who were close to being atheists. What linked them all was a common belief in the sacredness of all human life, in the equality of all men and women, regardless of their skin color or background.

At Northampton Sojourner met, for example, Giles Stebbins, a Unitarian minister; Samuel Hill, a businessman who became an ardent abolitionist after hearing Wendell Phillips speak; the community's leader, George Benson; David Ruggles, the freeborn black man who had edited an antislavery paper in New York before old age and blindness had brought him to the care of his Northampton friends. She also met the two great figures of the abolitionist movement, William Lloyd Garrison and Frederick Douglass.

William Lloyd Garrison had been born in Massachusetts in

Engraving showing Sojourner Truth
as a young woman

1805 and at the age of twenty-three became involved in the abolitionist movement. His ideas on the subject evolved rapidly, and soon he was advocating a more violent response against slavery than had previously been given by the early antislavery movement. His position led to his arrest and brief imprisonment in 1830, an experience which resulted in his even greater adherence to the cause of abolition. In 1832 he formed the New England Anti-Slavery Society, the first to call for the immediate emancipation of all slaves, and a year later was in Philadelphia for the founding of the American Anti-Slavery Society. His newspaper, *The Liberator*, earned him both wide acclaim and bitter criticism, for in it he trenchantly expressed his militant views against slavery. First published on January 1, 1831, *The Liberator* appeared regularly, overcoming grave financial problems by means of the generous support of the free black population who ardently backed Garrison. The controversial nature of his editorials angered the supporters of slavery but provided inspiration for those who fought against the system. The first edition of the paper carried his uncompromising declaration: "Urge me not to use moderation in a cause like the present. I am in earnest—I will not equivocate—I will not excuse—I will not retreat a single inch—AND I WILL BE HEARD."

Frederick Douglass had been born into slavery in Maryland, in 1817. His mother was black, his father white. In 1840 he escaped and went to Baltimore, where he worked and taught himself to read and write. When Sojourner Truth met him, he had been free only four years. In later years he was to become a highly respected public figure. Then, as now, he was hailed as the greatest black leader of his period; he was an eloquent and fiery speaker, blending fluency with conviction when he spoke on many subjects in addition to slavery and abolition. Because he had escaped from bondage, there was always the danger he would be recaptured, and in 1845, shortly after meeting Sojourner, he left for Europe. He spent two years there before he returned, a completely free man: friends in England had paid his purchase price of $750 and thus bought him his liberty. He worked tirelessly for the cause of abolition, participating also in the movement for women's rights. After emancipation he was honored in Washington, and eventually served in various diplomatic capacities in Santo Domingo and Haiti, as well as at home. The mark he made on his period is immeasurable, and Sojourner Truth was to encounter him or his ideas and thoughts at many junctures in her long life.

Unfortunately, Douglass has not left an account of the first time he and Sojourner met at the Northampton Association. In those days she was not as well known as she would later become, and more than likely the young Douglass was too involved in talking with the more prominent people he met there to notice the tall black woman. But the men and women Sojourner met at Northampton—Garrison, Douglass, and all the others—were articulate and forceful in their political and social convictions, and the conversations which she was able to hear must surely have influenced and changed her thinking.

An incident occurred during Sojourner's stay in Massachusetts which proved to be a further test of her strength of character. After her first few months in Northampton, she went to one of the association's camp meetings, held in a large, tent-dotted field. The services were interrupted when a crowd of noisy young men appeared, clearly intent on disrupting the proceedings and perhaps doing some violence. The leaders of the meeting urged them to leave and finally threatened them with the police. On hearing this, the rowdy men became incensed and shouted that they would burn down the tents and cause other damage.

Sojourner had hidden in the back of one of the tents, fearing for her safety, if not for her life. She was well aware that as the only black person in the meeting ground, she might well become the prime target of the young men's attacks, should a physical confrontation actually take place.

As she cowered in the tent alone, Sojourner began to ponder the situation and later on recalled that her thoughts ran something like this: "Shall I run away and hide from the Devil? Me, a servant of the living God? Have I not faith enough to go out and quell the mob. . . . I'll go to the rescue, and the Lord shall go with and protect me." With this she left the tent, in a state of great exaltation: "Oh, I felt as if I had three hearts! And that they were so large, my body could hardly hold them."

Alone, for none of the others would face the mob of young men, Sojourner walked to the top of a small hill on the meeting ground and began to sing. Her deep, melodious voice carried far, and the troublemakers turned and ran toward her as if to pull her down and silence her. As they approached, she stopped singing and asked them: "Why do you come about me with clubs and sticks? I am not doing any harm to any one." Disarmed by her tranquillity, they answered that they would not hurt her: "We came to hear you sing. Sing to us, old woman. Talk to us, old woman. Tell us your experience."

Surrounded by the roughnecks, Sojourner spoke to them and answered their questions. She even made them laugh. And they evidently enjoyed her singing, for they threatened bodily harm to anyone who might interrupt her. Finally she stopped and said to them: "Children, I have talked and sung to you, as you asked me; and now I have a request to make of you: will you grant it?" They assured her of their good will, and she asked them to leave in peace after she sang just one more song. True to their word, the men dispersed after hearing her sing, silently and without further trouble.

This experience marked an important stage in Sojourner's life, demonstrating the character traits that would carry her triumphantly through hostile confrontations in future years. She was firm and strong in dealing both with her own fears and with an angry mob; she acted decisively, yet with tact and modesty. When she left slavery, she did indeed leave behind the subservience and timidity which had been within her; she took with her only the core of will and strength upon which she never ceased to build for as long as she lived.

4.

I'll keep you scratching

After her experience at the Northampton community and her contact with the women and men involved in the abolition movement, Sojourner embarked on one of the campaigns which was to be of fundamental importance to her through her life: the struggle for the liberation of the black people of her country, both from bondage and from ignorance and poverty.

The decade leading up to the Civil War was a period of intense and impassioned activity on the part of all those Americans who believed in the words of the Declaration of Independence: "We hold these truths to be self-evident, that all men are created equal. . . ." The issue of slavery was becoming more and more tinged with violence, and government actions served only to aggravate the conflict between supporters and opponents of abolition. The Fugitive Slave Act of 1793, still on the books, was a virtual guarantee to any slaveholder that an escaped slave who was captured would be promptly and legally returned. As if this were insufficient, in 1850 Congress passed a "Compromise," one section of which was known as the Fugitive Slave Law. This infamous statute not only denied the escaping (or allegedly escaping) slave a trial by jury, but also forbade him or her to testify in court and made it a crime for anyone to assist in the escape. Finally, it included the proviso that it be retroactive and thus apply to most of the slaves who had escaped in the past.

With the passage of this law, hundreds if not thousands of blacks fled to Canada and Europe, knowing that it would make little difference to angry slaveholders and complacent judges if they were fugitives or not. For the kidnapping of freed or freeborn blacks had been a frequent occurrence through the earlier part of the century, and now, with the law so fully sanctioning the return of slave to master, it seemed likely that such abductions would increase.

The Fugitive Slave Law led also to increased militancy on the part of black and white abolitionists, who began to see that ending slavery would involve much more than mere speech-making and petitioning. Even respected public figures like Frederick Douglass now realized that violence might be the only feasible recourse in the fight for emancipation. Douglass was once moved by his outrage to declare that he would "welcome the intelligence tomorrow . . . that the slaves had risen in the South, and that the sable arms which had been engaged in beautifying and adorning the South, were engaged in spreading death and devastation."

Another harsh cry of wrath from this passionate man

Frederick Douglass

encountered the more pacific but equally fervent stance of Sojourner Truth. One day he spoke of the Fugitive Slave Law to an audience and asserted, "Slavery can only end in blood." In the back of the hall arose that dignified black woman. Ever earnest in her faith, she asked: "Frederick, Frederick, is God dead?"

"We were all for a moment brought to a standstill," recalled Douglass as he recreated the incident many years later, "just as we should have been if someone had thrown a brick through the window."

But indeed it did seem to many that Sojourner's kindly and egalitarian God was, if not dead, then at least absent, for the lot of the black American, enslaved or free, had scarcely improved during the first half of the nineteenth century. On the contrary, many laws and acts and compromises in addition to the Fugitive Slave Law made it less and less likely that the slaves would be freed, and even that the freedmen and women would remain so. The Missouri Compromise of 1820, for example, had given the slaveholding forces the entire Louisiana Purchase territory: Missouri and the region south of its southernmost boundary, as far west as what was then the westernmost frontier of the United States. And the Kansas-Nebraska Act of 1854 extended the territory open to slavery beyond the northern boundaries established in 1820, in effect repealing any of the antislavery segments of the original territorial compromise.

Most distressing of all legal decisions, perhaps because it so directly involved a human being and his survival, was the outcome of the Dred Scott case of 1857. Scott, a slave from Missouri, sued for his freedom when his master traveled with him from his home state into Illinois and Minnesota (both free territories) and then back again to Missouri. Scott argued that, having lived in free territories, he should be considered free, and that, according to the law, a resident in a free territory could not be enslaved. In one of the most lamentable decisions in its history, the Supreme Court ruled that since Scott (and therefore every slave) was not a citizen, he could not institute a court proceeding against another person. It further declared even the limited restrictions of the Missouri Compromise unconstitutional, thereby guaranteeing the absolute right of slaveholders to transport their human property anywhere they wanted at any time. Thus, all the territories were opened to slavery, and slaves were legally declared property with no human or civil rights.

The abolitionists, close to the pulse of antislavery sentiment in the country and alert to the machinations of the slaveholding lobbyists in Washington, were at all times prepared to escalate their struggle for the end of slavery. The earliest abolition groups, virtually all white, had been fundamentally religious and moderate and had supported a colonization plan which called for the settlement of free black Americans in colonies in Africa. But the new abolitionists were radical and militant; included in their ranks blacks and whites, women and men; and stood for immediate uncompensated emancipation and against colonization.

The new brand of abolitionism, loud and demanding, was born officially in 1833 when the American Anti-Slavery Society was formed in Philadelphia. This society and the scores of others which subsequently sprang up across the country undertook the task of bringing to all the American people arguments against slavery and demands for its abolition. Their efforts were seconded by the hundreds of women and men who spoke ardently to small and large gatherings in halls, churches, and courthouses. The period before the Civil War was also marked by eloquence in the written word, as antislavery journals and newspapers proliferated, and the biographies and autobiographies of ex-slaves became popular reading matter.

This was the atmosphere in the antislavery circle which Sojourner Truth joined wholeheartedly in the 1850s. Beginning with her lecture tours in the company of the British parliamentarian George Thompson, and through the period of her most active speech-making, she visited twenty-two states, covering thousands of miles, often on foot, in order to bring her truth to the people. She told anyone who would listen to her about the wrongs of slavery as she herself had endured them and about the rightness of freedom as she knew it and as her God ordained it. Her memories of slavery served her well in all her public appearances, drawing and holding audiences in rapt silence as the starkness of her words moved and angered them. Her background gave her speech a rough-hewn quality whose sincerity drew respect and admiration from even the most educated of listeners.

Sojourner never allowed herself to be intimidated or put down, rising to every occasion and gracefully withdrawing when she felt it judicious. The same courage she had displayed in Northampton when threatened by the obstreperous young men on the meeting ground was to show itself time and time again as she traveled through New York, New Jersey, Ohio, Indiana, Michigan, and all the other states she visited.

Blending tones of pride and modesty, Sojourner often addressed her audience as "children" and individuals as "honey," showing that affection for all sympathizers which endeared her to so many. And the salty wit already characteristic of her speaking style appeared on many occasions, as observers and listeners from the period recall. She was full of amusing sayings, some of which have survived and have been used by other speakers. On one occasion she began a talk by saying: "Children, I've come here like the rest of you to hear what I have to say," an opening gambit which a distinguished lecturer borrowed from her many years later. She coined her own characteristic aphorisms: instead of telling a dependent person to "stand on his own two feet," for example, Sojourner would urge that "every tub has to sit on its own bottom."

It was not only her humor and sharpness that made Sojourner an effective speaker against slavery, nor merely the fact that she spoke as one who had felt the whip's lash ("And now, when I hear them tell of whipping women on the bare flesh, it makes *my* flesh crawl, and my very hair rise on my head"). What also fast converted her into one of the most popular orators of the time was her ability to appeal to the better sentiments of white people by shaming them or encouraging them or even complimenting them. While Frederick Douglass and Harriet Tubman did the vital job of working with their own people, urging them forward and struggling by their side, Sojourner's role was somewhat different. She was one of the few black people of that period who spoke almost exclusively to whites, individually or in groups, and few blacks worked as closely as she did with the white abolitionists. The number of accounts which demonstrate her talent at subduing racist mobs and destroying racist arguments seem to confirm that she truly knew how to "deal with" white people of all persuasions.

One of her favorite reminiscences involved her "finding Jesus." She spoke of the questioning voice within her that

William Lloyd Garrison

wondered at her love for all creatures: " 'There's the white folks that have abused you, and beat you, and abused your people—think of them.' But then there came another rush of love through my soul, and I cried out loud—'Lord, Lord, I can love *even the white folks!*' " And indeed she could confront white people without rancor or bitterness, fear or timidity.

She must have been conscious of her power over white audiences, and clearly she took seriously her responsibility of convincing them to support her and her comrades in their calls for emancipation. At one meeting in Syracuse, in 1850, the crowd had come to hear George Thompson speak and were angered when Sojourner took the floor first. She quieted them by saying: "I'll tell you what Thompson is going to say to you. He's going to argue that the poor Negroes ought to be out of slavery and in the heavenly state of freedom. But, children, I'm against slavery because I want to keep the white folks who hold slaves from getting sent to hell." Sojourner's basic concerns undoubtedly involved her fellow blacks, but it is a testimony to her perceptiveness that she was able, at a difficult moment, to call forth such an astute statement. The meeting was saved, and the crowd listened to Sojourner and to Thompson with interest.

With Rochester as their headquarters, Thompson, Sojourner, and others traveled through western New York during 1851, speaking to audiences of various kinds. Many of these were unruly mobs whose only purpose was to disrupt the meetings and to fluster and perhaps injure the speakers. At all times, it seems, Sojourner maintained her dignity and never showed any fear before the greater strength and numbers of her opponents.

In 1853 her travels took her to the home of Harriet Beecher Stowe, author of *Uncle Tom's Cabin.* Written originally as a serialized novel and published only with reluctance by a Boston publisher, the book had sold 300,000 copies in the first ten months after publication in the United States, and 150,000 copies in England, bringing sudden and lasting fame to its author. (Lincoln even playfully called Stowe "the little lady who wrote the book that made this great war," referring to the Civil War.) So talked about was the novel, and so highly praised by all the activists in the abolitionist camp—while the proslavery forces were enraged by its revelations—that Sojourner soon heard of it, and became curious about its author. Sojourner finally found Stowe in Andover, Massachusetts, and the novelist has left to posterity a detailed account of their visit together.

Sojourner, arriving with a young grandson of hers, settled into the Stowe household with ease and pleasure, entertaining and surprising the other people gathered there with her singing, her preaching, and her reminiscing. Harriet Beecher Stowe wrote of her: "I do not recollect ever to have been conversant with any one who had more of that silent and subtle power which we call personal presence than this woman." Recalling her poise in that white, middle-class household of educated men and women, professors and preachers of renown, Stowe painted this picture of Sojourner: "She seemed perfectly self-possessed and at her ease; in fact, there was almost an unconscious superiority, not unmixed with a solemn twinkle of humor, in the odd, composed manner in which she looked down at me. Her whole air had at times a gloomy sort of drollery which impressed one strangely." And regretting the

Harriet Beecher Stowe

human loss occasioned by the enslavement of some human beings by others, she observed near the end of her article: "I cannot but think that Sojourner with the same culture might have spoken words as eloquent and undying as the African St. Augustine or Tertullian. How grand and queenly a woman she might have been, with her wonderful physical vigor, her great heaving sea of emotion, her power of spiritual conception, her quick penetration, and her boundless energy!"

As Sojourner Truth continued to travel, this energy carried her across the country, attacking slavery everywhere she went as inhuman, unchristian, and intolerable. She was understandably not always kind and moderate, and she was quite capable of giving vent to feelings of anger when she thought of what slavery had done. On one occasion she was quoted as declaring: "All the gold in California, all the wealth of this nation could not restore to me that which the white people have wrested from me." Although she claimed to be able to love the white people and to pity the slaveholder more than the slave, and even though her closest associates were white, Sojourner remained a spokeswoman for her people, never diluting her criticism of and opposition to the white society which had enslaved her and her fellow blacks. And this firm commitment to freedom and equality carried her over all those miles, bearing with her a white satin banner emblazoned with the words, "Proclaim liberty throughout all the land unto all the inhabitants thereof."

Her staunch belief in her truth enabled her to find retorts and answers when hostile listeners challenged her. Once in Ashtabula, Ohio, in 1855, she was sharing the podium with Parker Pillsbury, who had been sternly criticizing the church in America for its role in supporting the institution of slavery. He was then attacked by a young man in the audience who declared that blacks were closer to the animal kingdom than whites and thus were only useful as slaves. As a thunderstorm broke loudly outside, he went on to say that God was punishing Pillsbury and his adherents for the sacrilegious things he had said. Then Sojourner stood, and Pillsbury reports: "She seemed almost to come up out of the deep darkness or out of the ground. There she stood before us as a vision. Her tall, erect form, dressed in dark green, a white handkerchief crossed over her breast, a white turban on her head . . . a spectacle weird and fearful as an avenger—doubtless to the young man more dreadful than the thunderstorm. . . ."

Sojourner turned to the man who had derided Pillsbury and said in her deep, calm voice: "When I was a slave away down there in New York, and there was some particularly bad work to be done, some colored woman was sure to be called on to do it. And when I heard that man talking away there as he did, almost a whole hour, I said to myself, here's one spot of work sure that's just fit for colored folks to clean up after." Then, after reminding her listeners that she was proud of being pure African in her descent, without a drop of white blood in her, she remarked that the young man should not fear that the storm was God's wrath: "Child, don't be scared; you are not going to be harmed. I don't expect God's ever heard tell of you."

Whatever the rhetorical circumstances, Sojourner had an extraordinary talent for bringing the talk back to slavery. How, she wondered, could those with the power and the opportunity to speak and be heard, talk of anything other than that burning issue while families were still being separated, children being sold away from their mothers? On one occasion, when a religious speaker had been extolling the virtues of family love, Sojourner rose majestically, tears streaking her face. Speaking metaphorically rather than literally, she cried out: "We have heard a great deal about love at home in the family. Now, children, I was a slave, and my husband and my child were sold from me. . . . Now, husband and child are *all* gone, and what has become of the affection I had for them? *That is the question before the house!*"

She saw herself, then, as a sort of reminder or conscience for those who would wander away from what mattered. As long as she could keep the issue alive, keep people's minds on it, she was doing her job. When a northern Ohio man said rudely to her one day, following a meeting, "Old woman, do you think that your talk about slavery does any good? Why, I don't care any more for your talk than I do for the bite of a flea," Sojourner answered with tremendous conciseness and not a little salt: "Perhaps not, but the Lord willing, I'll keep you scratching." And that was what she did. She made people uncomfortable unless they were tackling the problem of slavery and its abolition.

Once she heard someone praise the Constitution and its provisions for equality and justice for all. Sojourner compared that document to the insect-infested wheat of the fields: "Now I hear talk about the Constitution and the rights of man. I come up and I take hold of this Constitution. It looks mighty big. And I feel for my rights. But they aren't there. Then I say, 'God, what ails this Constitution?' And you know what He says to me? God says, 'Sojourner, there's a little weevil in it.' "

In praising as well as in attacking, her remarks were to the point and could be touching or devastating. When a lawyer in the audience at a meeting stood and ranted about the blacks being nothing more than apes and baboons, Sojourner managed to bring the audience's scorn upon him when she replied: "Children, I am one of those monkey tribes. . . . I am going to reply to this creature. Now in the course of my time I have done a great deal of dirty scullion work, but of all the dirty work I ever done, this is the scullionest and the dirtiest. Now, children, don't you pity me?"

She also spoke gently at times, as when she addressed the Children's Mass Meeting at the Methodist Church, during the Annual State Sabbath School Convention in 1863. Facing the young, all-white audience, she said: "Children, who made your skin white? Was it not God? Who made mine black? Was it not the same God? Now, children, remember what Sojourner Truth has told you and thus get rid of your prejudice and learn to love colored children, that you may be all the children of your Father in Heaven. . . ." Her words often succeeded in dissipating the remnants of prejudice and hatred which might have existed at the meeting she was addressing. "She produced a singular effect upon the audience," wrote a New Yorker in 1868, "melting away the prejudice of color and creed. We have seldom witnessed more marked results upon the Soul of an audience. . . ."

Throughout the articles reporting Sojourner's "lectures" and other activities in support of abolition, references are often made to

Eminent opponents of the slave power

her encounters with "Negro-haters" and "mobocrats," loud-voiced, insolent opponents of black freedom who tried over and over again to disrupt her meetings and drown out her truths. Some of these clashes are described by eyewitnesses, others merely alluded to. Perhaps the most gripping series of confrontations took place in Indiana, where she traveled in the company of the abolitionist Josephine Griffing.

Indiana was a border state, which was at the time undecided on the slavery issue; but clearly the proslavery Democrats were in the majority where lawmaking was concerned, for there were statutes making it illegal for blacks to enter the state and others forbidding white people to entertain blacks in their homes. When it was known that Sojourner Truth, the noted lecturer and outspoken opponent of slavery, a black woman, was coming to speak, mobs formed and crowds gathered, attempting to stop her meetings from being held. On one such occasion, there were threats to burn down the hall in which she was scheduled to speak; hearing this, Sojourner loudly declared that she would speak on the ashes if necessary.

Sojourner and her friends were arrested several times: she for entering and remaining in the state, they for welcoming her into their homes. In each case she managed to outwit the authorities or simply to shame them into releasing her. At one point Union soldiers had to protect her from arrest by the local police; another time the prosecution lawyers, drunk when they entered the courtroom, took one look at the crowd of influential friends surrounding Sojourner, and left again, to be seen entering the tavern across the street!

Sojourner's meetings in Indiana were loudly and insultingly disrupted by shouts of: "Down with you! We think the niggers have done enough! We will not hear you speak! Stop your mouth!" The situation became so fraught with danger that for one meeting Sojourner's friends decided to outfit her in military regalia in order to put the fear of God into her enemies. As she later recalled it, "The ladies thought I should be dressed in uniform as well as the captain of the home guard. So they put upon me a red, white, and blue shawl, a sash and apron to match, a cap on my head with a star in front, and a star on each shoulder. When I was dressed I looked in the glass and was fairly frightened. Said I, 'It seems I am going to battle.' My friends advised me to take a sword or pistol. I replied, 'I carry no weapon; the Lord will preserve me without weapons. I feel safe even in the midst of my enemies; for the truth is powerful and will prevail.' "

Thus dressed, she was taken to the meeting in a carriage, surrounded by armed soldiers. The mob that was gathered around the courthouse, where she was to speak, stood firm at first, but upon seeing the crowd of supporters following Sojourner's carriage, they rapidly dispersed, "looking like a flock of frightened crows, and not one was left but a small boy, who sat upon the fence, crying, 'Nigger, nigger!' " The meeting proceeded as planned, and this time without interruption.

One of her most revealing confrontations also occurred in Indiana and was reported to William Lloyd Garrison by an abolitionist friend who had witnessed it. Wishing to find some means of discrediting Sojourner before she spoke, Democrats in Silver Lake circulated a rumor that she was in fact a man in disguise, a Republican spy sent by the antislavery people to spread dissension in the community. The third meeting she held there, in the hall of a sect called the United Brethren, was attended by a large proslavery crowd led by a Dr. T. W. Strain. At the end of the meeting, this man stood up and asked for silence. He declared that the majority of the people present believed the speaker was a man and felt it just that she allow several women from the crowd to examine her breasts in order to confirm or deny this belief.

In the midst of the tumult that ensued, Sojourner arose and asked above the noise why it was they suspected such a thing. "Your voice is not the voice of a woman, it is the voice of a man, and we believe you are a man," was the answer. Dr. Strain called for a vote to determine whether or not Sojourner was a man, and the ayes won!

The climax of this scene is best described by the eyewitness: "Sojourner told them that her breasts had suckled many a white babe, to the exclusion of her own offspring; that some of those white babies had grown to man's estate; that, although they had sucked her colored breasts, they were, in her estimation, far more manly than they (her persecutors) appeared to be; and she quietly asked them as she disrobed her bosom, if they, too, wished to suck!"

This, then, was the lecturer against slavery, the statuesque, dark, rich-voiced woman who traveled far and wide to spread the truth about slavery and the call for freedom. She was fearless in the face of danger, biting in her wit, sharp in her attacks, pointed in her arguments; tender when necessary, but never weak. As she promised the man who questioned her relevance, she kept the nation scratching at a time when too many people were silent in the presence of the unspeakable wrongs of slavery. Sojourner Truth also joined the ranks of her white sisters in another fight for human justice, when she saw the undeniable link between black rights and women's rights.

5.

If women want rights, why don't they just take them?

In 1840 William Lloyd Garrison found himself in London as one of the American delegates to the World's Anti-Slavery Convention. Among his co-delegates were two women, Lucretia Mott and Elizabeth Cady Stanton, well known in their country as dedicated and militant abolitionists. The convention organizers refused to seat the two women, on the grounds that members of the female sex could not serve in such a capacity, and told them to take spectators' seats in the balcony. Their male comrade-in-arms went with them, refusing, with these words, to participate in the convention: "After battling so many long years for the liberties of African slaves, I can take no part in a convention that strikes down the most sacred rights of all women."

Wendell Phillips, representing the sentiments of all the male delegates from the United States, also supported the women by introducing a motion to seat them. In arguing for his motion, Phillips made the parallel between sexual discrimination and racial discrimination: "When we have submitted to brickbats and the tar-tub and feathers in New England rather than yield to the custom prevalent there of not admitting colored brethren into our friendship, shall we yield to parallel custom or prejudice against women in Old England?" Unfortunately, the motion was defeated, and Wendell Phillips joined Garrison and the two women as a spectator.

This experience was to bear much fruit. Not only did it clarify for the men the need for reforms within the antislavery movement, but for Mott and Stanton it served as the impetus for the creation of the women's rights movement.

Though women were excluded from performing important functions and holding positions of responsibility within the abolition movement, they constituted a vital part of it. The women were charged with raising most of the funds that kept the movement going; they petitioned for emancipation, helped the schools for black children, and also took to the roads as traveling lecturers for the cause. There were women who were important links in the chain known as the Underground Railroad, involved in the dangerous activity of smuggling escaping slaves into New England or Canada.

The public activities of the women abolitionists soon brought down on them the scorn of established institutions, the churches in particular. Mounting scathing attacks on the women who spoke and traveled in the company of men, the defenders of Christian virtue often waxed poetic in condemning them, as in the pastoral letter where woman was compared to the fruits of nature: "If the vine, whose strength and beauty is to lean upon the trellis work and half conceal its clusters, thinks to assume the independence and over-shadowing nature of the elm, it will not only cease to bear fruit, but fall in shame and dishonor in the dust."

We have seen that even in the bosom of the abolition movement women were regarded as less than full participants, despite their tireless work. At the meeting of the American Anti-Slavery Society in 1833 women had been neither seated nor invited to sign the Declaration of Sentiments. This slight to the female membership resulted in the formation in Philadelphia later that year of the Female Anti-Slavery Society, only a few months after its sister group was founded in Boston. From 1837 on there were annual meetings of the Anti-Slavery Convention of American Women, and their work in the movement was increasingly vital. But despite their efforts, at the 1840 convention in London women were once again denied their rightful place beside the male abolitionists.

The energetic participation of women in abolitionism, as well as these attacks, seems to have crystallized for most women who opposed slavery the whole issue of women's rights. Not least articulate among these feminist abolitionists were black women, who recognized all too poignantly the double jeopardy under which they lived, as members of both the subject ethnic group and the subject sex. The black women formed the focal point at which the two struggles became one, and the white women working toward abolition also saw plainly the extent to which the struggle they

Lucretia Mot

waged for others was identical with that they must wage for themselves.

The opponents of abolition just as readily opposed feminism, and very often on similar grounds. They found just as many biblical quotations to prove women's inferiority as to prove that of blacks, always ending with the contention that both blacks and women were by nature dependent and childlike, needing the constant guidance, attention, and direction of white men. Popular mouthpieces in the press were quick to pick up these arguments and produced many that were as circular and idiotic as this one: "How did woman first become subject to man, as she now is all over the world? By her nature, her sex, just as the Negro is and always will be to the end of time inferior to the white race and, therefore, doomed to subjection; but she is happier than she would be in any other condition, just because it is the law of her nature."

The same women who gave so unsparingly of their time and energy to the abolitionist movement came together on July 19, 1848, in the Methodist Church at Seneca Falls, New York, to hold the first Woman's Rights Convention. In the Declaration of Sentiments resulting from the meeting, the women and men gathered there protested that "the history of mankind is a history of repeated injuries and usurpations on the part of man toward woman, having in direct object the establishment of an absolute tyranny over her," and went on to list the ways in which men had maintained this despotism over women. The document concluded with the demand that women, one-half the population of the United States, be admitted forthwith to full citizenship, and with the promise that all those present would not rest in their work until such equality between the sexes had been fully and firmly established.

Among the resolutions put forward by the chairwomen was one calling for the legal enfranchisement of women. Interestingly enough, only one man in the convention supported that call for woman suffrage: Frederick Douglass. His eloquent appeal on behalf of his sisters brought about the narrow majority needed to pass the suffrage resolution. Only ten years out of slavery, this young man had the perception to recognize that women must be granted their legal and constitutional rights within the society just as blacks must. Forty years later he was to recall: "There are few facts in my humble history to which I look back with more satisfaction than to the fact, recorded in the history of the Woman Suffrage movement, that I was sufficiently enlightened at the early day . . . to support your resolution for woman suffrage." With his characteristic modesty he continued: "I have done very little in this world in which to glory, except this one act. When I ran away from slavery, it was for myself; when I advocated emancipation, it was for my people; but when I stood up for the rights of woman, self was out of the question, and I found a little nobility in the act."

After 1848, doubtless inspired in part by Douglass's act of support, meetings of black abolitionists and the series of Negro Conventions held throughout the period almost always included black women among their delegates. The admiration and respect of most black male abolitionists for the women who worked with them must also have contributed to the relatively early emergence of this policy of sex equality. Black women, too, spoke out on the question, and as early as 1827 the black newspaper *Freedom's Journal* printed a letter from an anonymous black woman in which she appealed for extended education of her sisters. Douglass's paper *The North Star* frequently carried announcements of women's conventions and meetings and articles discussing and praising the work of women as abolitionists and as feminists. Douglass, Garrison, and other men who openly espoused the feminist cause were derisively called "Aunt Nancy Men" or "hermaphrodites," but this did not make them less proud to be thus associated with the women who fought for their rights.

However, not everything was harmonious within the antislavery movement. There was friction between the supporters of women's rights and those who were concerned only with the ending of slavery. In fact, some believed that the appearance of female speakers before "promiscuous audiences" (as the mixed gatherings were called) would alienate potential supporters of abolition, although the women more often than not had proved to be the most entertaining, articulate, and effective of the orators.

In 1840 the differences on this issue led to a split within the abolitionist movement. Lucretia Mott and Lydia Maria Child were elected to serve on the executive committee of the Anti-Slavery Society, the first women ever to be considered for such a responsible position. Lewis Tappan, a dedicated abolitionist but opposed to women in the leadership, declared that "to put a woman on a committee with me is . . . contrary to the usages of civilized society" and led the group which split with the society. This conflict between the "pure" abolitionists and the male and female feminist-abolitionists was to continue until late in the century, when the issue of suffrage once again brought it to the fore.

If women want rights, why don't they just take them?

Sojourner Truth came upon the feminist movement at about the same time she was introduced to abolitionism. During her stay at Northampton, she met and listened to men and women who were active in both causes and was soon moved and convinced by what they said. By the end of her life as an agitator for black and women's rights, Sojourner had met and befriended almost all the major figures in the women's movement. The autographs and letters that she collected attest to the esteem in which these feminists held her: Susan B. Anthony, Lucretia Mott, Lydia Maria Child, Josephine Griffing, Elizabeth Cady Stanton, Frances Gage, and Nannette Gardner.

One of the first times Sojourner was present at a Woman's Rights Convention was in October, 1850, in Worcester, Massachusetts. As she later retold the experience to Harriet Beecher Stowe, Sojourner sat for a long time listening to Frederick Douglass, Lucy Stone, Wendell Phillips, William Lloyd Garrison, and Ernestine Rose speak about women's rights. She soon became intrigued, and when called upon to speak she presented her position quite concisely: "Sisters, I aren't clear what you be after. If women want any rights more than they got, why don't they just take them and not be talking about it?" For Sojourner, it was obvious that action was more effective than words.

This aggressive approach often brought Sojourner the mistrust or criticism of those who saw her behavior as inappropriate to a woman. Even her supporters and admirers often praised her for what they saw as "manly" virtues and traits. In fact, when she was still Isabella, her master Dupont had boasted that she worked as well as any male fieldhand on his farm, if not better, since she also did the laundry! Yet this "masculine" woman was praised also for those qualities considered "feminine": gentleness, compassion, kindness. When we think of the woman who bared her breasts before an audience of hostile males questioning her right to speak, it should not surprise us that Sojourner Truth took so naturally to the feminist struggle, for to her that blend of strength and gentleness was precisely the essence of true womanhood.

However, Sojourner was not blindly supportive of everything her feminist colleagues did and said, and her salty retorts were appropriately pointed when it came to her criticisms of the women's movement. When some women asked her with surprise why she did not join them in wearing bloomers (a daring breach of feminine etiquette among middle-class matrons, who were supposed to remain dainty and doll-like in flounced and lacy dresses), Sojourner replied that she had had enough of bloomers when she was a slave. "You see," she explained, "they used to weave what they called nigger cloth, and each one of us got just such a strip and had to wear it width-wise. Them that was short got along pretty well, but as for me. . . ." This was a humorous, wordless reference to her great height. "Tell *you,* I had enough of bloomers in those days."

On another occasion Sojourner attacked the frivolity of women's fashions. With biting humor, she spoke of the "mothers and gray-haired grandmothers" who wore "panniers and Grecian-bend backs and flummeries . . . high-heeled shoes and humps on their heads." She called for a reform of women's dress, thinking it essential if the serious business of women's rights was to be discussed with any effectiveness: "What kind of reformers are you, with goose-wings on your heads, as if you were going to fly, and dressed in such ridiculous fashion, talking about reform and women's rights. It appears to me, you had better reform yourselves first."

But in general Sojourner found herself in full agreement with the positions taken by her co-feminists. She was an ardent advocate of women's rights on the most diverse of platforms, taking every opportunity she could find to raise some question on the subject, just as she did with the burning issue of slavery. Papers from Kansas, New Jersey, Massachusetts, and many other states reported on her speeches on women's rights and female suffrage, quoting her as pointing out that since men had done such a poor job of governing the world, it would make a great deal of sense to let women have a try, since even God seemed to want it so: "Did Jesus ever say anything against women? Not a word. But he did speak awful hard things against the men."

Not all the audiences she faced were friendly, but as she had proved time and time again when speaking in favor of abolition, Sojourner's eloquence and sharp wit could quell the disruptions of hostile crowds. In 1853 she was present at the Woman's Rights Convention held in the Broadway Tabernacle in New York. The hall was packed with hecklers and opponents of women's rights; chroniclers of the movement referred to that meeting as the "Mob Convention," so unruly and vociferous were their enemies during the session. When Sojourner rose to speak, and the crowd saw her color, the din was even greater.

She opened her remarks by referring to the noisy audience as people with either the spirit of geese or that of snakes. She

This cartoon mocked the aims of the women's rights movement, predicting its victory would bring in "The Age of Brass."

proceeded to speak above the uproar and finally managed to quiet the crowd: "I know that it feels a kind of hissing and tickling like to see a colored woman get up and tell you about things, and Woman's Rights. We have all been thrown down so low that nobody thought we'd ever get up again; but we have been long enough trodden now; we will come up again, and now here I am."

She continued her address by drawing upon the biblical tale of Queen Esther and King Ahasuerus, a story in which the woman comes forward to ask for her rights, just as women in the nineteenth century were doing. "When she comes to demand them, don't you hear how sons hiss their mothers like snakes, because they ask for their rights; and can they ask for anything less? . . . But we'll have our rights; see if we don't; and you can't stop us from them; see if you can. You may hiss as much as you like, but it is coming. Women don't get half as much rights as they ought to; we want more, and we will have it." As she concluded, Sojourner chided her detractors in the crowd for "hissing like snakes and geese," and reminded them that Jesus had required them to honor both father and mother. As usual, her speech was a resounding success.

At the Woman's Rights Convention in Akron, Ohio, held a year later, Sojourner outdid herself as an orator for women's rights. Although no formal records were kept of her words, we are fortunate that her friend and companion Frances Gage felt it important to write them down as she recalled them.

Gage prefaces her account of the occasion by remarking that "the [feminist] cause was unpopular then." Indeed, in those days, as the feminist and abolitionist Angelina Grimké wrote, for the conservatives "womanhood seem[ed] to be as objectionable as . . . abolitionism." The antagonism of so many Americans to the women's rights movement caused many of its followers to fear public appearances and confrontations, and often the conventions and meetings were dominated by male speakers who would take the opportunity to attack the women's platform rather than support it. So it was not surprising that the timid organizers of the meeting in Akron were none too happy when the majestic black woman entered the hall, wearing her familiar Quaker-style gray dress and "uncouth" bonnet.

Sojourner walked up the aisle to take her seat on the corner of the pulpit steps, seemingly oblivious to the murmurings that Gage heard all too clearly: "An abolition affair! Woman's rights and niggers! We told you so! Go it, old darkey!" During the intermission the fearful women begged Frances Gage, in her capacity as chairwoman, not to allow Sojourner to speak, in case people thought that the woman's righters were getting involved in abolitionism.

Not until the second day of meetings did Sojourner take the floor. After hearing the men in the crowd, all of them respectable clergymen of the Methodist, Baptist, Episcopalian, Presbyterian, and Universalist churches, she felt moved to speak. For those honorable gentlemen, claiming to have the truth from Jesus Christ himself—through the Bible—denied the justice of the women's struggle. They backed their claims by pointing out that Christ was a man and by arguing that "if God had desired the equality of woman, he would have given some token of his will through the birth, life, and death of the Savior." Others declared that men were intellectually superior to women and therefore entitled to broader rights; still another reminded the women that it was Eve and not Adam who had caused man's expulsion from Paradise.

"Slowly from her seat in the corner rose Sojourner Truth," reported Gage. "She moved slowly and solemnly to the front, laid her old bonnet at her feet, and turned her great, speaking eyes to me." Despite the urgent pleas that she not be allowed to speak, her friend the chairwoman announced Sojourner as the next speaker, and this is what she said:

"Well, children, where there is so much racket there must be something out of kilter. I think that 'twixt the niggers of the South and the women at the North all talking about rights, the white men will be in a fix pretty soon. But what's all this here talking about?" And then she addressed herself directly to the men who had spoken earlier:

> That man over there says that women need to be helped into carriages, and lifted over ditches, and to have the best place everywhere. Nobody ever helps me into carriages, or over mud puddles, or gives me any best place, and aren't I a woman? Look at me! Look at my arm! I have plowed, and planted, and gathered into barns, and no man could head me—and aren't I a woman? I could work as much and eat as much as a man (when I could get it), and bear the lash as well—and aren't I a woman? I have borne five children and seen them most all sold off into slavery, and when I cried out with a mother's grief, none but Jesus heard—and aren't I a woman?

Sojourner continued speaking, to a hushed crowd which now and then burst into applause as she demolished one after another of the clergymen's arguments. On the question of Christ's manhood she pointed out that, be that as it may, Christ was born "from God and a woman. Man had nothing to do with him." And in defense of her foremother, Eve, Sojourner declared, "If the first woman God ever made was strong enough to turn the world upside down, all alone, these together ought to be able to turn it back and get it right side up again, and now they are asking to do it, the men better let them."

Her reasoning had won the meeting over, silencing even those who might still disagree and giving encouragement to the timorous women who at first had opposed her speaking. In ending her report of that session, Frances Gage says of Sojourner's timely appearance: "She had taken us up in her strong arms and carried us safely over the slough of difficulty, turning the whole tide in our favor. I have never in my life seen anything like the magical influence that subdued the mobbish spirit of the day and turned the jibes and sneers of an excited crowd into notes of respect and admiration."

Once again, in the very center of the fiery battles of the day, Sojourner Truth proved that she was more than a match for the irrational and inhumane forces of reaction. Valiant warrior that she was, she downed her enemies when and where they appeared, moving on past them with the dignity and majesty of a truly free woman.

6.

I sell the shadow to support the substance

Sojourner Truth's first biography, her *Narrative*, appeared in 1850. It was one of a series of such works written or dictated by ex-slaves during the nineteenth century as a vehicle for exposing the evils of slavery and inspiring decent Americans by the example of their lives. Frederick Douglass's *Narrative* is one of the best known of such works. Although self-educated, Douglass had a natural gift with language that rendered the words of his autobiography powerful enough to survive the passage of time, and it is still widely read today. Sojourner, however, was not as fortunate as Douglass: she was illiterate all her life, although it is said that in her waning years she attempted to learn to read and write. Had it not been for the generosity and interest of two white women, we might never have been able to read her own account of her experiences and feelings.

NARRATIVE

OF

SOJOURNER TRUTH;

A Bondswoman of Olden Time,

Emancipated by the New York Legislature in the Early Part of the Present Century;

WITH A HISTORY OF HER

LABORS AND CORRESPONDENCE

DRAWN FROM HER

"BOOK OF LIFE."

BATTLE CREEK, MICH.:
PUBLISHED FOR THE AUTHOR.
1881.

Title page of a late edition of Sojourner Truth's *Narrative*

The first was Olive Gilbert. A New England woman who knew some of the horrors of slavery from her visits with Southern relatives, she clearly saw in Sojourner's oral reminiscences the seeds of a book. The two women met at the home of George Benson, a man who had befriended Sojourner during her stay in Northampton and had invited her to live at his home when the association disbanded. The meeting took place in 1847, when Sojourner was fifty. Gilbert heard her recount the stories and memories from her childhood as a slave, and listened also to the account of that strange relationship between the unlettered black woman and the fanatic "prophet" Matthias.

Familiar with Douglass's *Narrative*, which had caused quite a scandal with its detailed listing of names and places in the horror tale of Southern slavery, Olive Gilbert felt that, though slaves in New York had been emancipated only twenty years previously, there were still Northerners who chose to ignore the past existence of slavery in their communities. She knew that a book telling Sojourner's experiences as a slave in the North would shake the complacency of many a New Englander who might be enjoying a false sense of superiority over the Southerners who still practiced slavery. Gilbert was also moved by the sincerity of Sojourner's faith, being a strongly religious woman herself, and she felt that the black woman's unshakable belief in God's goodness and her devotion to doing His work would serve as a moral lesson to skeptics.

So Olive Gilbert not only took down Sojourner Truth's own words, but also sought out her friends and acquaintances and questioned them about their contacts with Isabella and later with Sojourner. She incorporated their observations and memories into the text of her book and filled it out by including letters which Sojourner had received and the written testimonials to her honesty and industry which she always carried with her. Through the good graces of a Dr. James Boyle, the money to print the *Narrative* was collected, and in 1850 a book of about 130 pages appeared.

This *Narrative* covers Sojourner Truth's life only up to 1849, ending with a visit she paid to her old master, John Dumont. It brings her to the time just after she left Northampton and therefore does not describe her entry onto the battlefields of abolitionism and feminism. However, thanks to Frances Titus, a white woman whom Sojourner met in the 1860s in Battle Creek, Michigan, the later editions of the *Narrative* were expanded. Titus added a preface and afterword, bringing the account up to date, as well as newspaper articles and letters which even further round out the portrait of Sojourner Truth.

The *Narrative* went through six editions. The second, in 1853, comprised only the original text, with a preface by Harriet Beecher Stowe. The third edition, in 1875, was issued at Frances Titus's expense and included not only an introduction by William Lloyd Garrison, but also the additional two hundred pages of material gleaned from Sojourner's several scrapbooks and called, like them, "The Book of Life." The last edition, published in 1884, one year after Sojourner's death, included also Titus's description of her last days, her illness, her death, and the funeral.

In her introduction to the second edition, Harriet Beecher Stowe made it quite clear that Sojourner intended to sell the book wherever she could, in order to support herself. "Her object in the sale of this little work is to secure a home for her old age, and the kind-hearted cannot do better than to assist her in this effort." For many years, traveling in the company of her abolitionist and feminist companions, Sojourner did indeed sell the book and was thus able to live and also to save a small amount.

She had long wanted to purchase land and a house, and had already done so in 1850: on the strength of future sales of the *Narrative*, she bought from Samuel Hill a small lot in Northampton, originally part of the association. She must for a time have intended to live there. But her spirit seemed to prefer the excitement and variety of a life on the move, and she stayed only a short time in her new home, preferring to continue her itinerant lecturing. It was after having purchased that small house that she joined the British abolitionist George Thompson in his travels through the country; it was also afterward that she went to Rochester, attended the various women's rights conventions, and traveled and worked in and around Salem, Ohio, for several years. In fact, it was quite clear that only when her legs refused to carry her any longer would Sojourner settle down in one place.

In the course of her wanderings during the 1850s Sojourner met, among scores of like-minded people, the Quaker Henry Willis, from Michigan. He lived in a town which, because of a fight on the banks of the river between some contractors and two Indians, had come to be called Battle Creek. At that period the black population of Michigan hardly reached six thousand, and in 1850 only fifty-four black citizens were counted in Battle Creek. But it was a town whose population was known for its antislavery sentiment, and it even boasted a section of the Underground Railroad which was manned by the town's Quaker mayor.

Sojourner spent some time there and seemed to like it, for after a short absence she returned and boarded with the Merritt family, friends of Garrison, Parker Pillsbury, Wendell Phillips, and other abolitionists. In the autumn of 1857 she returned to Northampton to speak and sell copies of the *Narrative*; while there, she also sold her property for $750. With the money she went back to Michigan and bought land and a small house in Harmonia, a spiritualist community only a few miles from Battle Creek.

By the beginning of her Michigan days, Sojourner Truth was entering her sixties, although there were rumors circulating that she was closer to eighty. She still bore her nearly six feet well, standing straight and proud. By then she was wearing steel-rimmed glasses, and she continued to sport the Quaker-style dresses, the turban and bonnet which so many observers described.

Apparently ready once again to settle down, by 1860 Sojourner was joined in Harmonia by her daughter Elizabeth Banks and two grandsons, James Caldwell and Sam Banks. A little later another daughter, Diana Corbin, moved there with her husband Jacob. While her children looked after her home, Sojourner, by now nationally known as a lecturer, continued to travel, visiting Ohio, Indiana, Iowa, Illinois, Wisconsin, and other parts of Michigan during the late 1850s and early 1860s.

It was no surprise that Sojourner chose Battle Creek as her home during her later years. She seemed to prefer it even to Harmonia, for when she was ill in 1863 she chose to stay at the Battle Creek house of her friends the Merritts, rather than with her children in Harmonia. Once she was stronger, she moved to a small wooden house on College Street, built by the generosity of her

Frances Titus, Sojourner Truth's
Battle Creek friend and traveling companion

friends. In 1867 the deed to that building was signed over to her, and it became her home until her death.

While Sojourner was in Battle Creek in 1863, a traveling photographer took her portrait, and soon she found another way to support herself. She had the picture printed up on cards, and underneath appeared the caption: "I sell the shadow to support the substance." Through the sale of these *"cartes de visite,"* as they were called, and the continued sale of the several editions of her *Narrative*, Sojourner was able to subsist, although she was never particularly well off, and at times her finances were extremely shaky. Whenever she wanted for anything, however, there were loyal friends who came to her aid, sending her money and clothing and seeing to it that she was cared for as she grew older and her health began to fail her. As she put it, "The Lord manages everything."

In Battle Creek Sojourner was revered, for she was the first citizen of national renown to settle there. It was there that she met Frances Titus, who soon became her "manager," caring for Sojourner's needs, organizing her lecture tours and often accompanying her, handling her correspondence, and publishing the several editions of the *Narrative.* Battle Creek's most illustrious citizens were proud to be Sojourner's friends, and even after her death those who had known her were considered fortunate. It is said also that Battle Creek's children loved her and would gather on her front porch, as she sat smoking her white clay pipe, and ask her to tell them stories. Always eager for an audience, Sojourner would willingly entertain the children. She liked them to read to her from the Scriptures, preferring children to adult readers who tended to

Sojourner Truth's *"carte de visite*

I Sell the Shadow to Support the Substance.

SOJOURNER TRUTH.

interpret the Bible for her. "Children," explained Frances Titus, "as soon as they could read distinctly, would re-read the same sentence to her, as often as she wished, and without comment."

Some members of Sojourner's family eventually joined her in the house on College Street in Battle Creek, while others stayed on in the house in Harmonia. Of all her daughters, the best known in Battle Creek was Diana Corbin, the eldest. She resembled her mother quite closely in appearance, being tall and gaunt and dark-complexioned. After Sojourner died, Diana was to pose for a posthumous portrait of her mother seated with President Lincoln.

Her two other daughters, Sophia and Elizabeth, lived and died with their families in Michigan; little more is known of them. Their children, Sojourner's grandsons, led quiet lives also, although of them we have more details. William Boyd, the grandson who had been with Sojourner in 1853 when she visited Harriet Beecher Stowe, became an engineer for a stationary engine in Battle Creek but died quite young of tuberculosis. James Caldwell, another grandson, fought with an all-black regiment during the Civil War. And Sammy Banks, Sojourner's favorite grandson, traveled often with her in her later years; his death in 1875 was a tremendous blow to her and marked the beginning of a real decline in her health.

While Sojourner Truth was widely known and honored during her lifetime and after, her family was curiously obscure, leaving few traces for posterity. Sojourner's fame would wane for a time as well, although her memory was maintained in the minds and words of the men and women who worked by her side. It is from them that we learn, for example, of the causes Sojourner espoused during the last decades of her life, causes which focused more and more on improving the daily existence of black people and securing civil and political rights for them and for women.

7.

I'm going down there to advise the president

As the nineteenth century advanced, resistance to slavery grew and spread, so that violence against slaveholders and their property became frequent. As a further attempt to preserve the institution of slavery, efforts were made to suppress the details of slave uprisings; in fact, until quite recently, most history books carried very little information about slave rebellions. The impression was given that the slaves by and large did not mind their condition, except in those cases of exaggerated cruelty by a master. Now we know otherwise, for it has been documented that consistently, from as early as 1526, slaves in the United States fought against their own enslavement.

Thus, while abolitionists agitated against slavery and conductors on the Underground Railroad smuggled slaves out of bondage, many who remained in servitude showed their opposition to the slave system by rebelling violently against it. Historians have unearthed irrefutable evidence of close to two hundred slave uprisings before the Civil War; there were undoubtedly a great number of others, if one is to judge from the numerous indirect references.

As the war approached, revolts occurred with increasing frequency, and the explosive situation culminated in 1859 when a white man named John Brown, at the head of a small integrated group, attacked the federal arsenal at Harpers Ferry in Virginia, in an attempt to capture the arms stored there and use them to free the slaves in the area. The assault failed, and Brown and most of his men were either killed in the battle or executed later for treason.

John Brown's daring assault terrified the slavocrats, whose fears had been steadily increasing with each reported slave rebellion. There were those who chose to see Brown merely as an exception, a fanatic, a madman who had somehow managed to convince a handful of dupes that his lunatic plan would work. Those slaveholders with clearer vision, however, recognized that Brown's act was symptomatic of a profound change in the mood of slavery's opponents. They realized all too sharply that from then on they would not merely be dealing with speakers attacking their right to own human beings, but with armed men and women who would physically challenge that right.

Following the attack on Harpers Ferry, and up to Brown's execution on December 2, 1859, the slaveholders on the one hand became more desperate than ever, and the abolitionists on the other were unwavering in their sympathy for Brown and his companions. The New England philosopher and war resister Henry David Thoreau, for example, referred to Brown as "a man such as the sun may not rise upon again in this benighted land," while Garrison, Phillips, Douglass, and others all openly praised him and mourned his death.

Clearly, those who supported slavery would have to change their tactics, for both blacks and whites were becoming increasingly daring in their resistance, and the slaveholders began to feel threatened. In the spring of 1860 the proslavery majority in the Senate passed a series of resolutions to ensure the flowering of slavery in the territories, hoping thereby to strengthen their position in the country as a whole. Imagine their horror and outrage when Abraham Lincoln, a candidate supported by the recently formed Republican party, won the presidential election in that year. While this new party did not run its candidate on an antislavery platform, it was clear that Lincoln's victory meant the decline of Southern control of government: the Republican party represented the Northern industrialists and businessmen, whose interests differed sharply from those of the Southern planters. Although the Republicans opposed slavery only in the territories and seemed willing to protect the right of each state to regulate its own institutions, the abolitionists backed Lincoln in the presidential campaign, a fact which further enraged the already threatened slave owners.

Lincoln took office on March 4, 1861. By that time, seven Southern states had seceded from the Union, in flagrant defiance of the newly elected president. Intent on preserving the United States as one nation, Lincoln sought to hold the remaining eight slave states by avoiding all actions which might alienate them. But on April 17 the slaveholders, angered beyond endurance, attacked Fort

Sumter in South Carolina, and the Civil War began. When Lincoln moved against the attackers, four more states seceded and joined with the others to form the Confederate States of America under President Jefferson Davis.

Although Lincoln had at first been cautious, hoping to placate the irate slave states, once the Civil War broke out he made it somewhat more evident that slavery was one of the issues at the heart of the conflict. In 1849, when he was still a congressman, Lincoln had introduced a bill in Congress providing for the gradual emancipation of slaves in Washington, D.C. He had also opposed the opening up of the territories to slavery and had spoken against the Dred Scott decision. As president, he never openly espoused the position of the abolitionists, who called for immediate, total, and uncompensated emancipation; nevertheless, on July 4, 1861, Lincoln referred passionately to the Union's struggle "to elevate the condition of men—to lift artificial weights from all shoulders; to clear the paths of laudable pursuit for all; to afford all an unfettered start, and a fair chance in the race of life."

Sojourner Truth was in Michigan when the Civil War broke out. Although in her sixties, she was still active and was determined to make a contribution to the war effort. She had long trusted Lincoln, and when she heard the more radical abolitionists complaining that the new president moved too slowly on the slavery question, she is said to have replied disapprovingly: "Child! Have patience! It takes a great while to turn about this great ship of State."

Like Sojourner, most blacks in the North were encouraged by the fact that Lincoln was willing to go to war to oppose the slave states' secession, and hundreds tried to join the Union Army. Because there were no laws governing this eventuality, in most cases the black volunteers were refused. In New York the black men who wanted to fight began drilling and training on their own, while they and others petitioned Washington for permission to join the army. By the autumn of 1862 Lincoln finally yielded to this pressure, and a limited enlistment of black men was permitted. Full enlistment was not to occur until 1863, after the Emancipation Proclamation.

One of the people who had most actively urged the enlistment of black men in the Union Army was Frederick Douglass, and once the emancipation of the Southern slaves was accomplished, he urged his people to join up wherever they could. In a speech delivered in 1863, Douglass called on all black men in New York State to go to Massachusetts, where a black regiment had just been formed. He exhorted his listeners: "Go quickly and help fill up the first colored regiment from the North. . . . The case is before you. This is our golden opportunity. Let us accept it. . . . Let us win for ourselves the gratitude of our country, and the best blessings of our posterity through all time."

Two of Douglass's sons joined the 54th Massachusetts Volunteer Infantry (Colored), and so did Sojourner Truth's grandson James Caldwell. The proud grandmother felt a pang of envy, for her impulse was to march alongside him and fight the evils of slavery even on the field of battle. As she put it, James had "gone forth to redeem the white people from the curse that God has sent upon them," and she wished she could be there too: "I'd be on hand as the Joan of Arc, to lead the army of the Lord. For now is the day and the hour for the colored man to save this nation." Sojourner recognized that the black population's commitment to the cause of freedom would give the Union struggle its greatest force and would ultimately secure its victory. When, after much delay, blacks were finally admitted to the armed forces, Sojourner remarked: "Just as it was when I was a slave, the niggers always have to clean up after the white folks."

All over the North, "colored" regiments were training, and Sojourner was able to contribute to the well-being of the fifteen hundred black troops in Detroit who, in 1863, enlisted in the 1st Michigan Volunteer Infantry (Colored). As reported in Detroit's *Advertiser and Tribune*, Sojourner visited the men at Camp Ward in November in order to cheer their spirits over the Thanksgiving holiday. She had gone among Battle Creek residents soliciting donations of food and money to provide the "boys" with a generous feast. As she approached one Battle Creek man, it is told, he rudely refused and spoke abusively of the war and the "niggers." When Sojourner asked him who he was, he answered: "I am the only son of my mother," to which she replied: "I am glad there are not more!"

Most Battle Creek residents, however, were more than generous, and when Sojourner went out to Camp Ward she took with her several large boxes filled with Thanksgiving delicacies. On her arrival, "the Colonel ordered the regiment into line 'in their best' for the presentation, which was made by Sojourner, accompanied by a speech glowing with patriotism, exhortation, and good wishes, which was responded to by rounds of enthusiastic cheers." After the official ceremonies, Sojourner remained with the men for

This picture of Sojourner Truth's visit with Abraham Lincoln was painted by Frank Courter after her death. Her likeness was copied from photographs, and her daughter Diana Corbin posed for the portrait.

several hours, talking and singing, giving them advice and comfort, and also helping to set up the dinner. So well received was she that before she left, the men made her promise to return on the following day and speak again.

Sojourner also composed a song for the Michigan Infantry and must have sung it to the volunteers during her Thanksgiving visit. The song, to the tune of "John Brown," embodied the deep patriotism of the men:

We are the valiant soldiers who 'listed for the war;
We are fighting for the Union, we are fighting for the law;
We can shoot a rebel farther than a white man ever saw,
As we go marching on.

They will have to pay us wages, the wages of their sin;
They will have to bow their foreheads to their colored kith and kin;
They will have to give us house-room, or the roof will tumble in,
As we go marching on.

Although the black soldiers proved themselves courageous in battle, they were subjected to humiliating and unfair treatment within the structure of the army. In July, 1863, the War Department had ruled that all black troops, of whatever rank, were to be paid the same as the fugitive slaves who were hired by the army to do menial labor. The black troops had white officers, generally inferior to those who led the white regiments; their weapons were old and in poor condition; they were given the most dangerous missions to perform or were simply assigned to unimportant noncombatant jobs.

Furious protests were lodged against this inequitable treatment; foremost in these outcries was the 54th Massachusetts Infantry. In a letter from a Corporal James Henry Gooding, their position and that of all the other black troops was eloquently stated: "We have done a soldier's duty. Why can't we have a soldier's pay?" During eighteen months of active duty, the 54th refused to accept any pay until they could be guaranteed pay on a par with that given to white soldiers! In September, 1864, Congress passed a special act awarding them $170,000 in full payment of their back wages since May, 1863, at the same rate paid to white troops. It was a great victory for the 54th and for all black regiments.

Unfortunately, Sojourner's grandson James Caldwell was not able to participate in the protest actions of the 54th, for he had been captured in South Carolina, on July 16, and his grandmother was notified that he was missing in action. He was not freed until 1865.

Seeing activity all around her, Sojourner could not long remain in Battle Creek, so far from the center of the upheaval. In the spring of 1864 she decided to go to Washington, even though she was by then close to seventy and had been in ill health the previous year. Without telling anyone, she made plans to leave in June, accompanied by her grandson Sam Banks. The day she was due to start on her journey, she went to the home where she worked as a laundress. As she scrubbed she said to her employer: "I've got to hurry with this washing, because I'm leaving for Washington this afternoon." The woman was surprised, and asked,

"For Washington? For goodness' sake, why are you going to Washington?" With her characteristic straightforwardness, Sojourner replied: "I'm going down there to advise the president."

With Sammy she traveled slowly across the country, stopping in Detroit, Brooklyn, New York, and in various communities in New Jersey, and in September she reached the nation's capital. Through the good graces of Lucy Colman, an abolitionist friend, Sojourner was granted an interview with Lincoln. The great day was September 29, 1864. A few months later Sojourner described the visit in a letter which she dictated to a friend: "It was about 8 o'clock A.M., when I called on the president. Upon entering his reception room we found about a dozen persons in waiting, among them two colored women. I had quite a pleasant time waiting until he was disengaged, and enjoyed his conversation with others; he showed as much kindness and consideration to the colored persons as to the whites—if there was any difference, more."

She went on to quote the first words she said to Lincoln: "I said to him, Mr. President, when you first took your seat I feared you would be torn to pieces, for I likened you unto Daniel, who was thrown into the lion's den; and if the lions did not tear you into pieces, I knew that it would be God that had saved you; and I said if he spared me I would see you before the four years expired, and he has done so, and now I am here to see you for myself."

The tall, gaunt man spoke courteously to the proud black woman who sat with him, as confident and poised as the most highly placed member of society. When Sojourner pointed out that before he ran for the presidency she had never heard of him, Lincoln answered with a smile: "I had heard of you many times before that." As for the rest of the interview, Sojourner reported: "I must say, and I am proud to say, that I never was treated by any one with more kindness and cordiality than were shown to me by that great and good man, Abraham Lincoln. . . . He took my little book, and with the same hand that signed the death-warrant of

Lincoln's autograph in Sojourner Truth's "Book of Life"

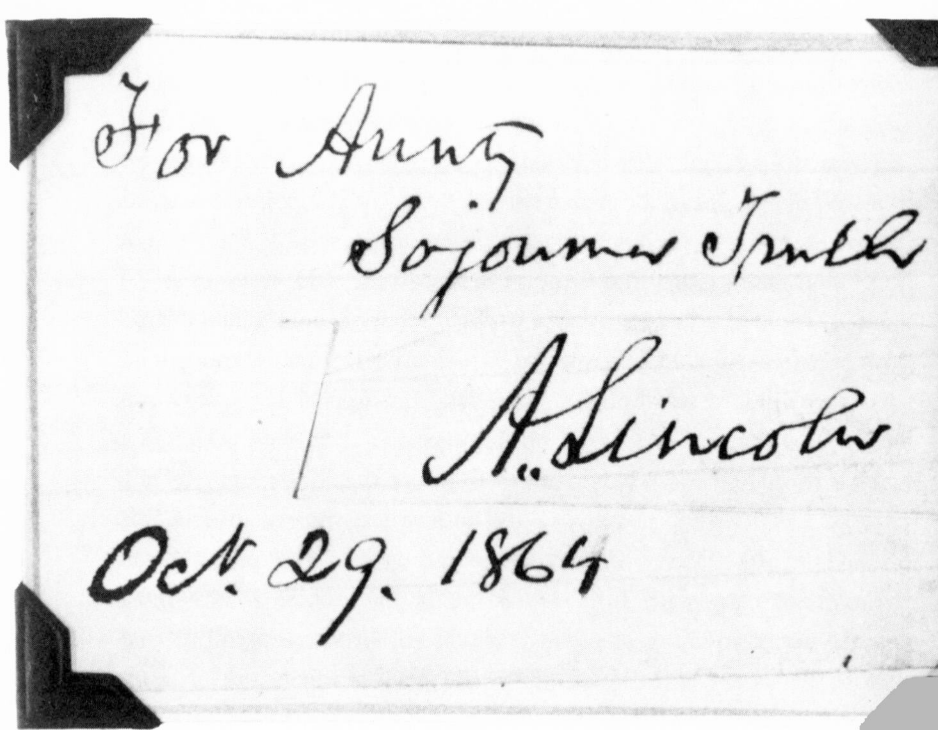
For Aunty
Sojourner Truth
A. Lincoln
Oct. 29. 1864

slavery, he wrote as follows: 'For Aunty Sojourner Truth, Oct. 29, 1864. A. Lincoln.' "

Indeed, it is for having signed slavery's death warrant that Lincoln is best known in our day, for the Emancipation Proclamation still stands as one of the most important documents in our history. So revered is the proclamation, signed on January 1, 1863, that we tend to forget that it provided for only partial emancipation, leaving in bondage about eight hundred thousand black people who were held as slaves in the areas of the country loyal to the Union.

While Lincoln's accomplishments were unquestionably major, all problems were by no means solved with the ending of slavery. Because the government had made no adequate plans for handling the influx of so many newly freed slaves into the cities, for training and housing them, for feeding them and providing them with medical attention, the settlements of ex-slaves in the North soon became urban slums.

And in the South things were no better. With the Emancipation Proclamation, the Confederate States determined to fight even harder. This determination was further toughened when, in January, 1865, the Thirteenth Amendment to the Constitution was passed by the House and sent to the states for ratification. This amendment abolished all slavery everywhere in the country. In retaliation, the Southern states passed the Black Codes, which were incorporated into each state's constitution with the express purpose of tightly regulating the lives of blacks in the South. Thus, although slavery was officially ended, black Southerners were now subject to restrictions almost as rigid as when they had been slaves:

they could not bear arms, they could not testify against white people, they had limited access to land and jobs. It was also in 1865 that the Ku Klux Klan was founded in Tennessee, beginning a long and bloody career as the major lyncher of blacks in the South.

Despite the Confederates' efforts to mobilize and maintain control of the South, by the summer of 1866 their forces were tremendously weakened, and on August 20 the Civil War officially ended. For the slaves who had been freed, the pleasures of liberty were sharply diluted by the harsh realities of a life of poverty and ignorance. No longer the property of other human beings, they were nevertheless not their own masters either, for not until 1868 was the Fourteenth Amendment ratified, granting citizenship to all black people. And the serious social and economic ills which prevailed in the settlements of ex-slaves and in the city slums continued to haunt those who took advantage of their hard-earned mobility and left the South, while those who remained there found it difficult to make a decent living.

Despite her advanced years, Sojourner Truth turned, at the end of the Civil War, to the job of helping her people make productive lives for themselves. There is no doubt that her visit with Lincoln inspired her greatly, and we can well imagine the deep pain she must have felt at his assassination on April 14, 1865. No one was ever to know what programs and laws Lincoln might have implemented had he lived, but Sojourner surely acted with him in mind when she gave herself over to the cause of the newly freed slaves. At times virtually alone in her battle, she strove to move the government to provide generously for the millions of black human beings whom it had freed from slavery.

8.

We have been a source of wealth to this republic

In his speech asking for black volunteers to join the 54th Infantry in Massachusetts, Frederick Douglass had spoken of his desire that black soldiers earn the gratitude of the government by their daring and courage. When her grandson joined that regiment, Sojourner Truth had declared that he was going to save white people from God's eternal damnation. In both these statements, the responsibility is somehow laid upon the shoulders of the black population; in the one case to earn the white world's thanks, in the other to atone in its place. In fact, the balance sheet should have read otherwise, for after so many centuries of labor violently wrested from them, of toil at harvesting and building, the black population should not have sought the government's nor anyone else's appreciation, but rather their just compensation for services rendered. This shift in emphasis occurred to Sojourner as she worked among the impoverished escaping slaves in and around Washington.

In 1865 the government finally recognized the crying need for social and economic assistance to the ex-slaves, who were attempting to build new lives and prepare themselves for jobs on the free market. Through the newly founded Bureau of Refugees, Freedmen, and Abandoned Lands, known simply as the Freedmen's Bureau, offices were set up all over the South to give clothing, food, medical help, shelter, and education to the ex-slaves. The bureau also helped them to find employment and protected them against exploitation by their new employers, who in their contract arrangements might well have attempted to take advantage of these men and women, most of whom were illiterate. The work of the bureau, massive in scale, was generally well done, among both whites and blacks: by 1867, forty-six fully equipped and staffed hospitals had been established in the South; between 1865 and 1869, 21 million food rations had been distributed; by 1870, over three hundred thousand refugees had been taken from the camps or the slums in which they lived and settled in communities where employment and adequate housing were available.

Yet the majority of the freed slaves had been accustomed to a rural life, and next to mobility, what most of them wanted was land. In 1862 General Rufus Saxton had recognized this when he mapped out a plan involving the area along the south Atlantic seaboard, then under Union control. Here he planned to allot two acres of land to each member of an ex-slave family who could till it and to provide tools and animals through cooperation with the government. In exchange, the family would grow corn and potatoes for its own consumption and in addition would produce a cotton crop for the government.

In 1864, General Sherman also proposed a solution to the land question when he issued an order that proclaimed a vast area of Southern land for the "exclusive settlement of the ex-slaves." Further, with the establishment of the Freedmen's Bureau had come the understanding that some amount of land would indeed be turned over to all those freed slaves who wanted it. Representative Thaddeus Stevens and Senator Charles Sumner both felt it just that the ex-slaves be repaid for their years of enslavement by being given land; Stevens proposed that from the 394 million acres confiscated from the largest Southern landowners, each freed slave be given forty acres, as well as a mule and agricultural implements.

But not all members of the government were in agreement with such an arrangement, for it seemed to some of them an infringement on the precious rights of property to redistribute the captured lands of Southern landowners. Among these were the conservatives who thought it unjust, and many of the more liberal men in Congress who, despite their previous sentiments in favor of ending slavery, felt that with emancipation the problems of the black population had been solved. Many of them simply did not understand what Sumner and Stevens were driving at. And so the granting of land to the men and women who had worked it, and whose ancestors had also worked it, was never accomplished.

Sojourner became passionately caught up in the battle to secure land for the ex-slaves. After her visit with President Lincoln, she had decided to remain in Washington in order to work more actively for the war effort. And there was much for her to do among the slaves who flocked there from the South. Ever since the first exchange of shots between Rebel and Union troops, thousands of slaves had fled their masters and moved toward the North. These people were officially referred to in the North as "contrabands," since they were considered captured enemy property. So harsh were the conditions under which they traveled and later lived, in the makeshift refugee camps set up by private and government agencies, that an estimated 25 percent of them died.

Those who managed to reach Washington or other cities fared little better, for there were no adequate accommodations for such large numbers of dispossessed people. During her stay in the nation's capital, Sojourner had ample opportunity to see firsthand the conditions of misery in which so many of them lived, herded into city slums, and late in 1864 she was officially commissioned to work with them. The document thus appointing her was one she was extremely proud of: "This certifies that the National Freedman's Relief Association has appointed Sojourner Truth to be a counselor to the freed people at Arlington Heights, Virginia, and hereby commends her to the favor and confidence of the officers of government, and of all persons who take an interest in relieving the conditions of the freedmen, or in promoting their intellectual, moral, and religious instruction."

Armed with this certificate, Sojourner was able to apply her ample talents to working with the inhabitants of Freedmen's Village in Virginia. Here she spoke to the freedmen, taught the women proper cleanliness and hygiene, and also became involved with their resistance to the kidnapping of their children by raiders from neighboring Maryland. On one occasion, when Sojourner

This Freedmen's Village in Hampton, Virginia, was similar to the village where Sojourner Truth worked among the newly freed slaves.

urged three women whose children had been abducted to turn to the law and get them back, the enraged kidnappers threatened to throw the old black woman into the guardhouse. Sojourner cried out that if they did, she would "make the United States rock like a cradle."

Less than a year later, because of her excellent work among the freedmen and women, Sojourner received an appointment to a hospital, this time from the Freedmen's Bureau. The officer in charge wrote of her: "Sojourner Truth has good ideas about the industry and virtue of the colored people. I commend her energetic and faithful efforts to Surgeon Gluman, in charge of Freedmen's Hospital, and shall be happy to have him give her all facilities and authority as far as she can aid him in promoting order, cleanliness, industry, and virtue among the patients."

Sojourner's twenty-six months in Washington were filled with a variety of activities. Frances Titus sincerely expressed her admiration for the energy and determination of this woman in her seventies as she wrote about Sojourner during her Washington days: "When we follow her from one field of labor to another, her time being divided between teaching, preaching, nursing, watching, and praying, ever ready to counsel, comfort, and assist, we feel that, for one who is nobody but a woman, an unlettered woman, a black woman, and an old woman, a woman born and bred a slave, nothing short of the Divine incarnated in the human, could have wrought out such grand results."

It must have been difficult work, teaching and counseling the poor people in the settlement and in the hospital. Although Sojourner herself left no descriptive reminiscences of the conditions under which the freed slaves lived, Frances Titus did include, in the section of the *Narrative* called "The Book of Life," a letter sent by Washington's superintendent of police to the Senate, describing several of the city's worst slum areas, almost wholly populated by "contrabands."

Speaking of a region known as "Murder Bay," for the high incidence of violence occurring there, he wrote: "Here crime, filth, and poverty seem to vie with each other in a career of degradation and death. Whole families, consisting of father, mother, children, uncles, and aunts . . . are crowded into mere apologies for shanties, which are without light or ventilation. . . . the atmosphere within these hovels [is] stifling and sickening in the extreme. . . . Some of the rooms are entirely surrounded by other rooms, so that no light at all reaches where persons live and spend their days and nights." Although the conditions in other areas might have been somewhat better than in "Murder Bay," nevertheless, "under the best sanitary laws that can be enacted, and stringently enforced, these places can be considered as nothing better than propagating grounds of crime, disease, and death; and in the case of a prevailing epidemic, the condition of these localities would be horrible to contemplate."

Sojourner Truth saw these squalid neighborhoods, and she worked with the people who were forced to inhabit them. She was deeply troubled by these sights, recognizing that epidemics and poor sanitation were only part of what faced the people in the slums, for crime, delinquency, lack of education, and inherited misery were sure to follow fast in such circumstances. She felt especially strongly that the young people, the children, ought to be moved elsewhere and be spared the fate which otherwise awaited them in those demoralizing slums. In order to help the freedmen and women escape from their lives of hardship, she went about finding homes for as many as she could in the North and on several occasions brought freed slaves directly from the South to Rochester, New York, where there were promises of housing and jobs from her many good friends in that city. In Washington she worked with

The Freedmen's Bureau issues rations to ex-slaves

General Howard toward the goal of having the government establish vocational and industrial schools, far from the city, to which the children of the ex-slaves might go to be educated and trained as productive citizens. Unfortunately, this project never materialized.

As she spent more and more time among those people whose lives had been used for the enrichment of others, whose labor had been stolen from them, whose children had been sold away, and who now were apparently to be abandoned to a fate almost worse than the one they had been freed from, Sojourner became angry. As she looked at the large, white buildings which beautified the nation's capital, she exclaimed: "We *helped* to pay this cost." And she went on, as Frances Titus later paraphrased it, detailing with painful accuracy the vast and various contributions the black people had made to the welfare and development of the United States, all of which had yet to be acknowledged and rewarded:

> We have been a source of wealth to this republic. Our labor supplied the country with cotton, until villages and cities dotted the enterprising North for its manufacture, and furnished employment and support for a multitude, thereby becoming a revenue to the government. Beneath a burning southern sun have we toiled, in the canebrake and the rice swamp, urged on by the merciless driver's lash, earning millions of money; and so highly were we valued there that should one poor wretch venture to escape from this hell of slavery, no exertion of man or trained blood-hound was spared to seize and return him to his field of unrequited labor. . . . Our nerves and sinews, our tears and blood, have been sacrificed on the altar of this nation's avarice. Our unpaid labor has been a stepping-stone to its financial success. Some of its dividends must surely be ours.

Bitter words spoken by a woman who herself had known the cut of the whip and the backbreaking field work that had indeed enriched the nation. Knowing of the vast lands owned by the government in the West, and knowing also that many, many acres were being given to the large and rapidly expanding railroad companies, Sojourner wondered why these acres should not go instead to the women and men whose bondage had served to increase the nation's wealth. She did not ask for all the land, merely enough on which to build a new life for the black people who so badly needed it.

Once again, this time in 1870, at the age of seventy-three, Sojourner Truth set out to speak before the most diverse audiences, stopping wherever she might be invited and bringing her observations to the people of the North and the West. As she traveled she also collected signatures of support for her proposed land grant for the freed slaves. Her petition was directed to the Senate and House of Representatives, and its final paragraph read: "We, the undersigned, therefore earnestly request your honorable body to set apart for them a portion of the public land in the West, and erect buildings thereon for the aged and infirm, and otherwise so legislate as to secure the desired results."

It was also during 1870 that Sojourner was able to visit with President Ulysses S. Grant, through an introduction from her friend General Howard. On March 31 she went to the White House, accompanied by Giles Stebbins from Detroit and several other people. Stebbins later recounted their meeting in the *Detroit Tribune*:

> She expressed her pleasure at meeting him, yet I could see it was not quite easy on either side. She had met Abraham Lincoln, and he, a born Kentuckian, could call her "Aunty" in the old familiar way, while Grant was reticent yet kindly. But

> a happy thought came to her. It was in the civil rights bill days, and not long before he had signed some act of Congress giving new guarantees of justice to the colored people. She spoke of this gratefully and the thin ice broke. Standing there, tall and erect while stirred in soul by the occasion, her wonderful eyes glowed with emotion as she thanked him for his good deed to the once enslaved race to which she belonged. . . . Words followed freely on both sides—she telling him how his tasks and trials were appreciated, and how much faith was placed in his upright doing of duty to the oppressed, and he quietly, yet with much feeling, expressing the hope that he might be wise and firm and never forget the inalienable rights of all.

The interview ended with Grant's signing Sojourner's "Book of Life" and choosing a photograph of her from among the various *"cartes de visite"* she had with her. They shook hands and she left. During this same trip to Washington, Sojourner visited the Senate chamber and was accorded a standing ovation by the legislators, after which many of them signed her book.

Unfortunately, we do not know whether or not Sojourner raised the question of the lands in the West with President Grant; perhaps such a topic was among the words which "flowed freely on both sides." In any case, on many occasions during the next few years Sojourner addressed large groups of people, hoping to win their support for her land proposal.

On January 1, 1871, for example, she spoke in Boston at a meeting of the National Association for the Spread of Temperance and Night Schools among the Freed People of the South. After describing her family and her experiences under slavery, an opening which she usually used when addressing a large crowd, Sojourner proceeded with "the question before the house": land for the freed slaves. She pointed out that there were people living in Washington at government expense, "costing you so much and it don't benefit them at all." And, as a paper reported it, she explained her plan for resettlement: "She wants the government, instead of feeding them as now, to put them on land of their own . . . and teach them to work for themselves."

She also spoke in Rochester, eloquently painting the picture of degradation in which the capital's black population lived. She went on: "You ask me what to do for them? Do you want a poor old creature who doesn't know how to read to tell educated people what to do? I give you the hint, and you ought to know what to do." She once again appealed for the granting of land by the government and for her audience's support for her petition. "You owe it to them," she exhorted, "because you took away from them all they earned and made them what they are. You take no interest in the colored people. . . . You are the cause of the brutality of these poor creatures. For you are the children of those who enslaved them." And then, recalling how eager people were those days to help the poor and oppressed abroad, she ended: "You are ready to help the heathen in foreign lands, but don't care for the heathen right about you. I want you to sign petitions to send to Washington. . . ."

Many of the newspaper reports of her speeches during this

period were friendly, but there were some which chose to abuse her for her outspoken support of unpopular causes and mock her uneducated speech and often unconventional ways. A paper in Springfield, New Jersey, went so far as to refer to her as an "old negro mummy," because of her advanced age, and claimed that "fifty years ago [she] was considered a crazy woman." The reporter strongly criticized the person who had brought Sojourner to the church in Springfield to speak, calling him a "pious radical" and complaining: "When respectable churches consent to admit to the houses opened for the worship of God every wandering negro minstrel or street spouter who may profess to have a peculiar religious experience, or some grievance to redress, they render themselves justly liable to public ridicule."

Another paper from Springfield declared: "We do most decidedly dislike the complexion and everything else appertaining to Mrs. Truth, the radical—the renowned, saintly, liberated, oratorical, pious slave. . . . She is a crazy, ignorant, repelling negress, and her guardians would do a Christian act to restrict her entirely to private life."

Despite such attacks, which served to show the seamiest side of the society in which Sojourner lived, she did not give up in her fight to get land for the indigent black people, although even the petition was unable to persuade the government to take her seriously. Her advancing age, her precarious health, and the threats and jibes of stupid people notwithstanding, Sojourner Truth continued to travel and preach, passing through Massachusetts, western New York, Michigan, Kansas, Iowa, Illinois, Missouri,

Wisconsin, Washington, Ohio, New Jersey, and Kentucky during the last ten years of her life. On all these trips she met with old and new friends, sang her songs, and continued entertaining and enlightening people on a variety of topics, all of which were intimately connected to the well-being and liberation of black people—and of women.

9.

I want to ride

In the first half of the nineteenth century disharmony grew within American society, and many social and political movements sprang up to right some of the wrongs which plagued it. The period during and after the Civil War witnessed an increased resolve on the part of all those involved in either championing or opposing the various causes. The outbreak of war between North and South made it impossible for anyone to continue ignoring the vital issues which moved the society, especially of course the question of slavery. For the reformers, the war tended to focus all efforts on the necessity for emancipation; the postwar period found many putting all their energy into winning guaranteed social and political rights for the newly freed slaves, almost to the exclusion of all other causes.

As Sojourner Truth threw herself into her work with the

ex-slaves, formulating and presenting her plan to settle interested freedmen on public lands in the West, she elicited little or no support from the Washington lawmakers. She was frustrated at every turn in her attempts to convince the men in power that her plan would work and would benefit both the black people directly affected and the nation as a whole. But the senators and congressmen were involved in other issues, and it became increasingly apparent to Sojourner that within the society there was a tremendous contradiction: those with the power to help her people were uninterested in doing so, and the people with a passionate commitment to social change (mainly blacks and women) were without power to effect it. She saw clearly that so long as the power to decide, the right to vote, was securely in the hands of white males exclusively, little would be done to alter the conditions of the people among whom she was working. Sojourner therefore became actively involved in the fight for black and woman suffrage.

The women and men at the Seneca Falls Convention in 1848 had voted by a narrow margin to fight for woman suffrage. The various groups of black women abolitionists had also on several occasions made it clear that in order to function effectively in the struggle they would have to be given direct political leverage, in the form of the ballot, along with the men. And during the early days of the women's movement, Frederick Douglass had come out strongly in favor of granting women the vote, pointing out that a well-run and effectual government must be founded on the intelligence of its citizenry and must use all the resources of wisdom and enlightenment at its disposal. "In this denial of the right to participate in government," he said, "not merely the degradation of woman and the perpetuation of a great injustice happens, but the maiming and repudiation of one-half of the moral and intellectual power of the government of the world." And he added, as Sojourner had also observed, that "seeing that the male governments of the world have failed, it can do no harm to try the experiment of a government by men and women united."

But the issue of woman suffrage was soon set aside, as the immediacy of black recruitment, the war effort, and black suffrage became increasingly compelling. Allowing no doubts as to their dedication, the women in the antislavery movement participated fully in these new struggles, feeling it appropriate for the time being that the emphasis be placed there.

In 1866 the Fourteenth Amendment to the Constitution was sent to the states for ratification, and some of its implications were thrilling to contemplate: "All persons born or naturalized in the United States, and subject to the jurisdiction thereof, are citizens of the United States and of the State where they reside." Citizenship meant political power, so it was said. But, it seemed that the persons referred to in the amendment were only those who were white and male. When the Fourteenth Amendment was passed, with its exclusion of women in the first section, and the actual use of the word "male" in the second (the only place in the Constitution where that word appears), many of the women were angered, feeling they had been betrayed by those men who had fought for the passage of that amendment. When the Fifteenth

Amendment was passed in 1868, guaranteeing the black male vote, the matter was clinched, for now women of both colors were clearly excluded from exercising the rights of citizens.

Around this issue developed a split in the suffrage movement. People like Susan B. Anthony and Elizabeth Cady Stanton felt that universal suffrage was the only possible and just platform on which to base a program, and others, like Douglass and Phillips, believed it important to secure the enfranchisement first of blacks and later of women. Those who withdrew from the fight for woman suffrage evidently did not realize that one-half of the black population whose political rights they championed would, when the battle for black male suffrage was won, continue to live in a position of powerlessness and dependence. Black women, having suffered the same cruelties under slavery as the men, having been forced to work at jobs which were as arduous and thankless as those done by the men, and having been subjected to the additional indignity of virtually unavoidable sexual abuse by white men, were forgotten in the hour of reckoning by both the white and the black men who now fought for racial equality to the exclusion of sexual equality. In retrospect, it seems a sad moment in the history of the movement for human justice.

But Sojourner Truth did not abandon her sisters, although she did not declare herself against the Fourteenth Amendment either. She continued in her quiet way to work for what she felt was right. In 1866 Susan B. Anthony wrote her a letter and enclosed in it a petition demanding certain rights for women, asking Sojourner to circulate it and find a sympathetic member of Congress who would present it on behalf of the disenfranchised women of the United

States. The fact that Anthony, a militant suffragist who as early as 1852 had been arrested for attempting to register to vote, should send such a petition to Sojourner shows that this black woman's views on the issue of woman suffrage were well known to the movement's highest leadership.

Indeed, Anthony did well to send her petition to Sojourner Truth, although as far as we know nothing ever came of it. For just as she had spoken in favor of women's rights and of the rights of freed slaves, she now gave herself over to advocating woman suffrage. At an equal rights convention in New York in 1867, Sojourner referred directly to the issue of universal versus partial suffrage. She interceded in favor of the black woman, heretofore ignored by the reformers:

> I feel that if I have to answer for the deeds done in my body just as much as a man, I have a right to have just as much as a man. There is a great stir about colored men getting their rights, but not a word about the colored women; and if colored men get their rights, and not colored women theirs, you see the colored men will be masters over the women, and it will be just as bad as it was before. So I am for keeping the thing going while things are stirring; because if we wait till it is still, it will take a great while to get it going again.

And Sojourner was right, for once the issue of woman suffrage was set aside in the nineteenth century, it was several decades before the next generation of feminists was able to force the question once again into the public consciousness.

Sojourner also brought in the question of equal pay for equal work: "I have done a great deal of work, as much as a man, but did not get so much pay. I used to work in the field and bind grain, keeping up with the cradler; but men doing no more, got twice as much pay. . . . We do as much, we eat as much, we want as much."

And then she pointed to the sad fact that she was the only black woman speaking out for black women's rights, and begged her listeners to join her. Addressing the men in the crowd, she said trenchantly: "You have been having our rights so long, that you think, like a slave-holder, that you own us. I know that it is hard for one who had held the reins for so long to give up; it cuts like a knife. It will feel all the better when it closes up again."

Sojourner felt strongly about the woman suffrage issue, and she not only spoke her feelings but also acted upon them. It is reported that she tried to vote for Ulysses S. Grant in 1868. Four years later, in Battle Creek, she attempted to register to vote in the third ward, where she lived. She was, of course, refused, but nevertheless she appeared the following week on election day and did her best to vote. Once again she was refused, but she remained at the polls all day, lecturing the authorities on the question of women's rights. The paper which reported this incident ended the article by saying, "It is Sojourner's determination to continue the assertion of her rights, until she gains them."

And that, indeed, is how she lived. She was absolutely resolute in her conception of what her rights were; whether or not the authorities agreed with her, she could do no less than attempt to exercise them. Her obstinacy about her right to vote moved

Elizabeth Cady Stanton to write in her "Book of Life": "I hope, dear Sojourner, that you will be enfranchised before you leave us for the better land." And it was not merely personal feelings that led her to fight to express her political opinion through the ballot; as in her fight for the end of slavery, she truly believed that she was doing the work of God and that somehow in her person and her actions was embodied all of God's will. Thus, when she addressed the equal righters in New York, she declared (perpetuating the myth of her great age): "I am above eighty years old; it is about time for me to be going. . . . I suppose I am kept here because something remains for me to do; I suppose I am yet to help to break the chain." Unfortunately, she was not to live long enough to see the day when women could vote, for the chain she referred to was only broken when the Nineteenth Amendment was finally passed in 1920, granting full suffrage to American women.

She was never discouraged in this fight. Not only did she make her own gestures toward exercising her rights, but she also encouraged others to do so. In 1871 she heard that her friend Nannette Gardner had actually succeeded in voting in Detroit. She asked for a written statement from Gardner to substantiate the story, and this letter she kept among her treasured autographs and papers until her death: "Dear Sojourner: —At your request I record the fact that I succeeded in registering my name in the First Precinct of the Ninth Ward, and on Tuesday, the 4th of April, cast the first vote for a state officer deposited in an American ballot-box by a woman for the last half century."

The energy and versatility of Sojourner, who fought for abolition, equality, and suffrage, moved her also into other fields of struggle. Like many feminists and abolitionists, Sojourner Truth was attracted to the movement for temperance, which called for voluntary abstinence from drinking alcoholic beverages. There are many references to her speaking before temperance groups, either on that subject itself or on the other questions that interested her. Like other black leaders, Sojourner Truth felt that alcohol was fast becoming a serious social problem among the black poor and believed that only complete sobriety would enable her people to pull themselves up fully from the mire of a past as slaves.

Chewing and smoking tobacco were also practices that were generally frowned upon by the reformers of the period. On one occasion, Sojourner was speaking before a temperance group in Kansas. All through the audience were men chewing tobacco and loudly spitting the brownish juice onto the floor. Finally unable to contain herself, Sojourner quipped: "When I attended the Methodist Church, we used to kneel down in the house of God during prayers. Now I ask you, how could anyone kneel down on these floors?"

She herself, however, smoked quite heavily during most of her life, and was rarely seen without her little white clay pipe. Her friends must have criticized her frequently for this habit, and once one of them reminded her that according to the Bible, "No unclean thing can enter the kingdom of Heaven," and that a smoker's breath was about as unclean as anything could get. Sojourner laughingly replied that when she went to Heaven, "I expect to leave my breath behind." Nevertheless, in her old age she was finally prevailed upon to stop smoking, and her Rochester friend Amy Post wrote joyously in a letter to the *National Anti-Slavery*

FREE LECTURE!

OJOURNER TRUTH,

Who has been a slave in the State of New York, and who been a Lecturer for the last twenty-three years, whose characteristics have n so vividly portrayed by Mrs. Harriet Beecher Stowe, as the African Sybil, deliver a lecture upon the present issues of the day,

On

l will give her experience as a Slave mother and religious woman. She es highly recommended as a public speaker, having the approval of many usands who have heard her earnest appeals, among whom are Wendell llips, Wm. Lloyd Garrison, and other distinguished men of the nation.

At the close of her discourse she will offer for sale her photograph and w of her choice songs.

A flyer announcing Sojourner Truth's lecture

Standard that though Sojourner "has been an inveterate smoker, she says from very early age, now she has laid it all aside, has not smoked once, in three months."

It is difficult to determine just what position Sojourner Truth took on the numerous other social issues of the period, for not much written testimony can be found. We can certainly speculate with some confidence as to what she felt about child labor, about working hours, and about war and peace. And we do have evidence that she was opposed to capital punishment, a subject on which she even addressed the Michigan State Legislature in her later years. A Battle Creek paper reported that she "made capital punishment advocates think they were not such capital fellows after all," by pointing out to them that "the person who wants to see his fellow beings hung by the neck until dead has a murderous spot in his heart." It is a pity we do not have more information regarding Sojourner's opinions on related social questions.

An important area in which she involved herself, which luckily was written up quite fully in "The Book of Life," was segregated transportation. Her confrontations with this occurred while she was working for the government in Washington, helping out among the freedmen and women. When she was serving at the hospital, she frequently had to ride the streetcars. She began to find it oppressive to be restricted to the blacks-only car, which was always packed with white people who did not want to crowd into the cars for whites only. It is reported that when she lodged a complaint with the president of the company, the segregationist policy on the trolley cars was officially ended.

Nevertheless, Sojourner had several more encounters with segregationist attitudes in the streetcars. One day she signaled a car to stop, and it passed her by. A second one followed suit, at which point she began shouting loudly: "I want to ride! I want to ride!" A crowd gathered around her, and soon the car she had been signaling was blocked by the traffic. With no more ado, Sojourner boarded it, to the great anger of the conductor. He told her to go up front or be thrown off. She sat down with dignity and pointed out that she was a passenger like any other. He repeated his threat, and she again refused to move, stating that the law was on her side. In order to strengthen her position, she rode on beyond her stop, finally getting off and happily declaring: "Bless God! I have had a ride!"

Her efforts to integrate the transportation system were not over, however. On another occasion a streetcar refused to stop for her, but she ran after it and managed to board it when it stopped to pick up some white passengers. When she chided the conductor for having made her run, he threatened to put her off. "If you attempt that," she cried, "it will cost you more than your car and horses are worth."

Another time it was her fellow passengers who gave her trouble. Sitting opposite some white women, she noticed them staring at her with great hostility. Finally one of them loudly asked the conductor, "Does niggers ride in these cars?" and he was obliged to answer "Yes." The women were angered, declaring it a shame: "They ought to have a nigger car on the track." At this point Sojourner spoke up, saying: "Of course colored people ride in the cars. Streetcars are designed for poor white, and colored, folks. There are carriages, standing ready to take you three or four miles for sixpence, and then you talk of a nigger car!" On hearing this, the women left the streetcar in a huff, presumably to take a more expensive and more exclusive conveyance.

Sojourner's friend and colleague Laura Haviland witnessed yet another incident involving the Washington streetcars. In this case the fact that Haviland, a white woman, was riding in the company of a black woman seemed to aggravate an already ticklish situation. In Sojourner's own words this is what happened:

> As Mrs. Haviland signaled the car, I stepped to one side as if to continue my walk and when it stopped I ran and jumped aboard. The conductor pushed me back, saying, "Get out of the way and let this lady come in." Whoop! said I, I am a lady too. We met no further opposition till we were obliged to change cars. A man coming out as we were going into the next car, asked the conductor if "niggers were allowed to ride." The conductor grabbed me by the shoulder and jerking me around, ordered me to get out. I told him I would not. Mrs. Haviland took hold of my other arm and said, "Don't put her out." The conductor asked if I belonged to her. "No," replied Mrs. Haviland. "She belongs to humanity." "Then take her and go," said he, and giving me another push slammed me against the door.

As a result of the conductor's physical abuse, Sojourner suffered a dislocated shoulder. This outrage led her to complain angrily to the president of the streetcar company. He seemed sympathetic to her plight, advising her to take the case to court, charging the conductor with assault and battery. She won her court case and the conductor lost his job. The victory was a great one for Sojourner, who rejoiced and declared, "Before the trial was ended, the inside of the cars looked like pepper and salt."

In many ways, Sojourner Truth gave herself wholeheartedly to the fight for justice and equality. She not only spoke out against inequity, she also risked her personal safety and literally put her body on the line whenever she was confronted with discrimination because of her sex or her color. The consistently principled stance she took on all the related issues of her century attests to her high degree of integrity and spiritual courage. The many important triumphs she experienced and the victories she won helped to make things just that much better for those who came after her.

10.

I'm going home like a shooting star

Four years before she died, a Louisville, Kentucky, paper wrote: "The oldest truth nowadays is Sojourner." And so it seemed, for it had been numerous decades since the nation first heard the name of Sojourner Truth. She seemed blessed with boundless energy, subject to rules of existence that were other than human; despite the great age she professed, she seemed never to tire and would pick up new causes to champion with a vigor unknown in most people of her years. But Sojourner was all too human, and her health had been declining as she approached the end of her life.

Of course, many of the people around her were misled as to her age, believing her to be almost a second Methuselah: one of them said that she was 82 as early as 1868; when she met with Grant and the senators in 1870, she was reportedly 90; close to death she herself declared that her age was 114, her obituary put it at 108, while on her gravestone, carved years later, appeared the age of 105. In fact, when Sojourner Truth died in 1883, she was 86 years old.

During her last twenty years her health had been poor, and we find in letters dictated by Sojourner reports on the progress of her recovery from one illness or another. In the *Anti-Slavery Standard* of February 13, 1864, appeared a letter in which she wrote: "Since I have been here [Detroit] I am gaining health and strength *fast*. . . . I can almost walk without a cane." A few years later a friend recorded in her diary that Sojourner's "health is quite good, she is cheerful and hopeful." Although Frances Titus wrote in the *Narrative*'s 1878 introduction that despite rumors of Sojourner's death, her "mind is as clear and vigorous as in middle age," she also reported that as far back as 1863 Sojourner herself had complained: "Lord, I'm too old to work—I'm too sick to hold meetings and speak to the people and sell my books." It is a further tribute to Sojourner's stamina and determination that she was able, in spite of ill health, to devote herself so selflessly to the various causes that occupied her during her final years.

Her decline truly began in 1874, when the illness of her favorite grandson Sammy depressed her deeply, and she too became ill with an ulcer on her leg. When Sammy died the following year, Sojourner's condition worsened, though a report in 1876 declared that she was by then "so much improved in health that she was leaving for Chicago and the Philadelphia Centennial." In the following few years she did travel with Frances Titus to New York, Chicago, and several other cities. But in 1883 the ulcers on her legs, which had long been plaguing her, finally worsened, and she took to her bed under the care of a friend, Dr. John Harvey Kellogg, the director of the Battle Creek Sanitarium.

A few days before she died, Sojourner Truth was visited by a journalist, and in his article he described her deathbed condition:

Some of the autographs in Sojourner Truth's "Book of Life"

Wendell Phillips
H B Stowe
Charles Sumner
Lucretia Mott.
L. Maria Child.
Geo Thompson
Gerrit Smith

Jonathan Walk
J. S. Griffing
Samuel J. Ma
O. O. Howard.
Rowland Johnsen
Lydia Mott
Amy Post

> In a half reclining position on a bed, her back bolstered up with pillows, . . . lay . . . Sojourner Truth. She said nothing until made aware of Mrs. Titus' presence, when she lifted her head slightly, displayed a great wrinkled and emaciated . . . face, but eyes as bright as they have ever been. Her illness . . . is very severe and causes her great pain. . . . and all hope is now given up of a restoration to health.

But even in pain, close to death, Sojourner was able to display that spirit which had become so familiar to her admirers and friends, and she spoke weakly with the visitor, mostly on religious subjects. She seemed completely at ease in the contemplation of her imminent death, feeling that God's glory was awaiting her. To a sorrowful friend who paid her a visit, Sojourner explained her serenity by declaring: "I'm not going to die, honey; I'm going home like a shooting star." Her deeply ingrained faith in God's goodness convinced her that she would return to the sky and go directly to His bosom. It was in this tranquil state of mind that Sojourner Truth died, at three o'clock on the morning of November 26, 1883.

She left behind her a host of mourning friends and thousands of other people who had never known her but had been touched by her words and by her deeds. All whom she reached, directly or indirectly, were deeply moved by her death, and the obituaries that appeared in papers throughout the North and the East were lavish in their praise for her contributions to the struggles of her time. A Battle Creek paper declared, "This country has lost one of its most remarkable personages," while a New York paper reminded its readers that she "did not seek the applause of her fellow beings" but worked quietly and with modesty.

More personal expressions of sadness came from her old colleagues Wendell Phillips and Frederick Douglass. The former wrote that Sojourner "was a remarkable figure in the anti-slavery movement, almost the only speaker in it who had once been a slave in a Northern state," and the latter that she had been "venerable for age, distinguished for insight into human nature, remarkable for independence and courageous self-assertion."

In Battle Creek her neighbors showed their sorrow by attending her funeral in large numbers (some claim that over one thousand people were present). Her casket was carried by the white residents of Battle Creek to the Congregational and Presbyterian Church there, where her friend Reverend Reed Stuart delivered the funeral sermon. She was buried in Battle Creek's Oakhill Cemetery.

Sojourner Truth's death came upon her quietly and unobtrusively, as a final punctuating episode in the long and fruitful life of this extraordinary woman. What mattered about her life was her life, not her death; the fact that she referred so rarely to her declining health indicates that she herself chose to ignore her mortality in order to continue her work among those who needed her most. For all who knew her or knew of her, she left a legacy of struggle and strength, the example of her determined faith in the ultimate victory of right over wrong.

During her lifetime a few tributes to Sojourner Truth were written, some surviving her into posterity. There was, for example, an essay, "The Libyan Sibyl," written by Harriet Beecher Stowe, in

Sojourner Truth's grave in Oakhill Cemetery, Battle Creek. Next to it stands a historical marker honoring her children and grandchildren buried nearby.

which Sojourner comes vibrantly alive in the novelist's descriptions. The *Narrative* and "The Book of Life," so carefully recorded, edited, and printed by Olive Gilbert and Frances Titus, are human documents in which the reader can sense the love and respect of so many of Sojourner's contemporaries.

The visual arts, too, paid tribute to Sojourner Truth. The sculptor William Wetmore Story, hearing Harriet Beecher Stowe's account of her meeting with Sojourner in her Andover home, was inspired to make a statue, which he called the *Sibilla Libica*. This work was shown in the World's Exhibition in London in 1862 and attracted much critical attention. And in 1892 Frances Titus commissioned a posthumous portrait of Sojourner, to be painted by the artist Frank C. Courter from the photograph on Sojourner's *"carte de visite."* The painting showed her seated with Lincoln, both of them looking at the Bible given to the president by the black residents of Baltimore. This painting was exhibited in the Michigan building at the 1893 World's Fair in Chicago and later hung in the Battle Creek Sanitarium until the building burned down in 1902. From a photograph of Courter's work, an artist named Jackson produced another canvas of Sojourner and Lincoln in 1913; it now hangs in the Detroit Historical Museum.

But beyond these memorials, and outside a faithful following among her colleagues and neighbors, few people carried Sojourner's memory actively into the twentieth century. Even in Battle Creek, where so many prominent residents had attended her funeral and where she was so often held up as the city's foremost and first famous citizen, her grave remained unmarked for thirty-three years, identified only as Number 9 in Lot 634. In 1904 the Daughters of the American Revolution launched a movement to have it properly marked. In 1916 a marble headstone was finally placed on the site. The inclemency of Michigan winters eroded it, and it was replaced in 1946 with the granite tombstone that today marks Sojourner's grave.

It was almost eighty years after her death before a historical marker was placed next to her grave by the Sojourner Truth Memorial Association of Battle Creek, commemorating her relatives who are buried nearby. This memorial association had been formed in the 1920s, and its project had been to raise five thousand dollars in order to perpetuate Sojourner's name. Dissolved during the 1930s, the group appeared later under different leadership and was responsible for providing the funds for both the historical marker and the Sojourner Truth Room in Battle Creek's Kimball House Museum. In Battle Creek there is also a Truth Drive which connects two streets in a housing project. And that city is the home of Berenice Lowe, a dedicated and meticulous historian who has devoted twenty years or more to researching Sojourner's life.

Battle Creek's loyalty notwithstanding, Sojourner Truth has not yet received the national attention she deserves, for outside of her home town not enough is known of her life. The Soldiers and Sailors Monument in Detroit shows the figure of a black woman crowning soldiers and sailors and is said to represent the black people's gratitude for emancipation. Legend has it that the black woman is Sojourner, but this has not been confirmed. At least two libraries in other parts of the country have rooms named for Sojourner Truth. And New York Congresswoman Shirley Chisholm visited her grave in April, 1972, an act of tribute by one black woman to another.

But there is no official memorial to Sojourner Truth in any of the other places she inhabited or visited. The place of her birth in

One of Battle Creek's present-day citizens models the dress allegedly sent to Sojourner Truth by Queen Victoria of England.

Ulster County, New York, is not marked, nor are the sites of her homes in Northampton, nor the various places she lived in during her years in New York City. Of all the schools in Detroit, in Battle Creek, in Boston, in Rochester, in New York—in all the cities whose decent citizens loved Sojourner so well during her lifetime—not one has been named in her honor.

There was one building bearing Sojourner's name. However, it attracted public notice not because it honored her memory, but because it served as the scene of a so-called race riot. In 1942 the federal government constructed a housing project in Detroit and named two hundred units of it the Sojourner Truth Houses. On February 28 of that year three black families were to move into the otherwise unoccupied buildings. They were prevented from doing so by a mob of twelve hundred whites armed with knives, bottles, clubs, rifles, and shotguns. In the fighting that ensued, police three times used tear gas to disperse the crowd; dozens of people were injured, and over one hundred were arrested. It was not until April, and then under the protection of eight hundred state troopers, that twelve black families were able to occupy their apartments.

Sojourner Truth, who believed above all in peaceful dialogue and energetic persuasion, would surely have wept to see the degree of intolerance that persists not a hundred years after her death. Had she seen the events of 1942, and others that since that year have screamed at us from newspaper headlines all over this country, she might well have wondered if her God was not, after all, dead. And today some might ask what it was all for, what Sojourner's years of sacrifice, her exhausting travels, her ardent words and courageous deeds have in fact accomplished.

Sojourner once said, "I never determined to do anything and failed." That belief is what is most essential about her life and is the only stance that is valid in the battle for human justice. From the moment she walked off John Dumont's farm, Sojourner Truth had absolute confidence in the rightness of her acts, in her ultimate triumph over the most imposing of obstacles.

Early in her life, when Isabella became Sojourner, she declared that her devotion to the truth would never die: "And truth shall be my abiding name," she promised. If Sojourner had not believed passionately in the justice of the struggle for black liberation, she would not have devoted her life to the cause of truth, and we would never have known her. Only by living ardently and fighting so that all people may be free can we earn the right to call her sister.

Index

About the Author

VICTORIA ORTIZ grew up in Mexico, Europe, and the United States. She received a bachelor's degree in French and Spanish literature from Barnard College and attended Brandeis University as a Woodrow Wilson Fellow. She has worked as a tour guide at the United Nations, a caseworker for various social agencies, and a high school and college teacher of French, Spanish, and Latin-American literature. She became interested in Sojourner Truth during the year she spent as a civil rights worker in Jackson, Mississippi, teaching history in various Freedom Schools.

Ms. Ortiz has received a Ford Foundation fellowship and is completing doctoral studies in comparative literature at the City University of New York. Her published writings include a number of translations and a book for young people, *The Land and People of Cuba.*